Why has the artist painted a date? What is the significance of the date itself? Is a date in white on a monochromatic canvas a work of art? As Anne Rorimer, a former curator of twentieth-century art at the Art Institute and now an independent scholar and curator, explains in her essay, Kawara uses his art (and his wry sense of humor) to examine time and its representation. What, the artist asks, is the nature of representing time, of isolating, identifying, and measuring moments?

One of Marc Chagall's masterpieces, the *White Crucifixion*, is the subject of our next essay. Ziva Amishai-Maisels, a professor of art history at the Hebrew University of Jerusalem, reveals that Chagall painted over parts of the original version of the *White Crucifixion*, thereby concealing imagery that openly condemned the Nazis for their persecution of the Jews. Professor Amishai-Maisels also examines in fascinating detail Chagall's use of Christian imagery in the *White Crucifixion* and other works, an element in Chagall's art that has seemed, for many observers, at odds with the artist's Jewish themes.

Our final essay focuses on the beautiful and ornate montage depicting the *Four Evangelists* that may have been created by Giulio Clovio. As Sandra Hindman, professor of art history at Northwestern University, and Michael Heinlen, assistant professor of art at Lake Forest College, have discovered, the Art Institute's montage was assembled from pieces of an illuminated manuscript that was created for Pope Gregory XIII and stolen from the Sistine Chapel in 1798, during the Napoleonic conquest of Italy. Through a combination of scholarship and detective work, Hindman and Heinlen have traced the origins of the Art Institute's *Four Evangelists*, and have, for the first time, placed it within the context of other fragments that were created by the same artist.

While the solution to the mystery of the *Four Evangelists* and its creator is elusive, Hindman and Heinlen's efforts are like those of our other authors—they greatly enhance our knowledge and appreciation of important works in the Art Institute's collection.

MICHAEL SITTENFELD
Editor

The
*A*rt *Institute*
of
Chicago MUSEUM STUDIES

VOLUME 17, NO. 2

The Art Institute of Chicago
MUSEUM STUDIES

VOLUME 17, NO. 2

Foreword   100

A New Attribution to Francesco Mochi   102
IAN WARDROPPER, *The Art Institute of Chicago*

The Date Paintings of On Kawara   120
ANNE RORIMER, *Chicago*

Chagall's *White Crucifixion*   138

ZIVA AMISHAI-MAISELS, *Hebrew University, Jerusalem*

A Connoisseur's Montage: 154
The *Four Evangelists*
Attributed to Giulio Clovio

SANDRA HINDMAN, *Northwestern University*

MICHAEL HEINLEN, *Lake Forest College*

Notes   179

Foreword

With this issue of *Museum Studies*, we turn our attention to the wide-ranging diversity of the Art Institute's collection in essays about the *Bust of a Youth* by the Italian Baroque sculptor Francesco Mochi, a painting by the contemporary artist On Kawara, the *White Crucifixion* by Marc Chagall, and a montage of fragments from a sixteenth-century illuminated manuscript.

Two of the essays examine works that have been difficult to attribute with certainty. In the past, a work of undeniable quality but obscure origin was often attributed to the most renowned artist of the time. But as our knowledge of an era and its artists has been expanded and refined, art historians have filled in many missing details. For centuries, Mochi's *Bust of a Youth* was thought to be the work of Gian Lorenzo Bernini, the most celebrated Italian sculptor of the Baroque era. And the Art Institute's montage of fragments, now known as the *Four Evangelists*, has been attributed in the past to the most influential painter of miniature works of the Italian Renaissance, Giulio Clovio. Our authors have sifted through many sources and much mitigating evidence to bring us to a fuller understanding of who created these works.

The mysterious origins of the *Bust of a Youth* and the *Four Evangelists* give way to other mysteries in this issue of *Museum Studies*. What, we may ask, was Chagall trying to say in his 1938 painting *White Crucifixion* about the persecution of European Jews during the Nazi era? Why did Chagall use avowedly Christian imagery to address the very real and immediate atrocities committed against the Jews? The work of On Kawara leads to very different questions, particularly with respect to his intentions. What, we might ask, has motivated Kawara to execute—over a period of almost twenty-five years—hundreds of "date paintings" that record simply the date of their making? And what, ultimately, can these paintings mean?

In our first essay, Ian Wardropper, Eloise W. Martin Curator of European Decorative Arts and Sculpture at the Art Institute, examines the work reproduced on our cover: Mochi's *Bust of a Youth*. Through a series of comparisons between works known to be by Mochi and others by his contemporaries, particularly Bernini, Wardropper establishes for the first time that the *Bust of a Youth* should be attributed to Mochi. In the course of his argument, Wardropper meditates on the beauty of Mochi's idealized image of a youth, and speculates that the sculpture might be a representation of Saint John the Baptist.

On Kawara's painting *Oct. 31, 1978* makes an indelible impression on the visitor to the Art Institute's galleries of contemporary art. As one looks at the large letters and numbers of Kawara's painting, a series of questions arise:

A New Attribution to Francesco Mochi

IAN WARDROPPER

Eloise W. Martin Curator of European Decorative Arts and Sculpture, and Classical Art

In the first decade of the seventeenth century, central Italy witnessed an artistic revitalization following the stagnation of late Mannerist painting, sculpture, and architecture. The painter Caravaggio employed explosive light and shade that splintered his canvases into dynamic compositions, while his intense realism and dramatic narrative riveted viewers. Annibale Carracci combined naturalism with grand, sweeping forms in the ceiling frescoes of the Palazzo Farnese, Rome. The architect Carlo Maderno enlivened the facade of the church of Santa Susanna, Rome, with a clearly directed progression of form. The sculptural equivalent of these early Baroque achievements is the early work of Francesco Mochi (1580–1654), whose well-known *Annunciation* at Orvieto (1605–08; figs. 2–3) plays the tense lines of the Virgin against the swirling movement of the angel; within this vortex of directional forces lies an unsettling psychological tug of war.

This proponent of a new sculptural dynamism produced relatively few works, so the identification of the *Bust of a Youth* (fig. 1) as the work of Francesco Mochi, proposed here for the first time, is significant. With the acquisition of this bust in 1989, the Art Institute added a masterpiece of Italian Baroque sculpture to its collections. The renewed appreciation among modern artists for Baroque dynamism and the awakening respect among historians for the role that Mochi played in its genesis add to the importance of the discovery of the *Bust of a Youth*.[1] To the sculptor's contemporaries, as the scholar Rudolf Wittkower put it, Mochi's *Annunciation* was "like a fanfare raising sculpture from its slumber."[2] In the judgment of art historian Howard Hibbard, "Mochi had been the first to break with the formulas that had stultified late sixteenth-century Roman sculpture...he is one of the

real heroes of early seventeenth-century art."[3] The taut linearism, dramatic movement, and subtle psychology of the *Bust of a Youth* are qualities of Mochi's work that have led recent historians to evaluate him as one of the most original and creative artists of the formative years of the Baroque.

To introduce this work into Mochi's oeuvre, we must place the bust within the artist's style as well as within the larger context of his age. First, a brief account of the sculptor's career will provide a basis to measure this bust against his best known work and to weigh evidence for the attribution. Second, an erroneous attribution to Gian Lorenzo Bernini (1598–1680) requires clarification of the two sculptors' opposing visions in order to discount the younger sculptor's authorship. Bernini so potently shaped the public monuments of Rome that his style has become virtually identified with Baroque sculpture. This state of affairs led to such indiscriminate ascription of works to Bernini that the former attribution to him of the *Bust of a Youth* is not surprising. But recent scholarly focus on Bernini, Mochi, Alessandro Algardi, and Francesco Duquesnoy, to name the

FIGURE 1. Francesco Mochi (Italian, 1580–1654). *Bust of a Youth (possibly Saint John the Baptist)*, c. 1630. Marble on variegated black marble socle; h. 40.5 cm (without base). The Art Institute of Chicago, Restricted gift of Mrs. Harold T. Martin through the Antiquarian Society; Major Acquisitions Centennial Endowment; through prior gift of Arthur Rubloff; European Decorative Arts Purchase funds (1989.1). This bust, previously attributed to Gian Lorenzo Bernini, is presented here for the first time as the work of Francesco Mochi. The masterful control of line and movement and the suggestive expression of the *Youth* are characteristic of Mochi's work, and make this an important addition to the Art Institute's collection of Baroque sculpture.

most prominent sculptors of the period, has made it possible to distinguish with greater accuracy among Italian Baroque sculptors.[4] A close look at the bust in relation to Mochi's and Bernini's work will clarify the complex evolution of the early Baroque. Finally, an examination of the identity of the subject, the type of work, and its possible function and patronage will help to establish the context of sculptural practice and Mochi's life.

Mochi's Career

Mochi was born in the town of Montevarchi. His artistic training began nearby in Florence, when he entered the studio of painter Santi di Tito. This artist favored simple composition and natural form, rejecting the complexity and artificiality of Mannerism. The pictorial clarity of Mochi's relief style, with its cut-out figures, seen around the base of his pair of equestrian monuments for the Farnese family in Piacenza (see fig. 4), testifies to the effect of his training in another medium. But it was the Florentine artistic milieu, with its emphasis on the primacy of design, more than the influence of one artist, that formed Mochi's art. The crisp line, angular bending of elbows and knees, and complex spatial movement developed by Giovanni Bologna and continued by such followers as Pietro Tacca shaped Mochi's austere linearity, sharply focused images, and nearly abstract purity of design.[5]

Around 1599, Mochi moved to Rome, the artistic capital of Italy in the seventeenth century, and he joined the workshop of sculptor Camillo Mariani. Only recently arrived from Venice, Mariani introduced emotional force and dramatic movement to Roman sculpture. Mariani's eight over-life-sized stucco saints in the church of San Bernardo alle Terme, Rome, break out of the confines of their niches to confront the spectator in a spatial strategy characteristic of later Baroque art. The deliberations on ecclesiastic reform at the Council of Trent completed in 1563 had promoted simple narrative in artistic works to make religious messages clear even to a non-literate congregation. The reticent hand-to-heart gesture of Mariani's statue of Saint Catherine of Siena in San Bernardo suggests her inner feelings, while the long drapery pleats exemplify the drive toward simplicity in the post-Tridentine period. Other sculptors of this generation, particularly Stefano Maderno, with whom Mochi worked on an important papal commission, the Capella Paolina in Santa Maria Maggiore, Rome, shared this new impetus toward simplicity. Maderno presented the recumbent figure of the dead Saint Cecilia (1600) in Santa Cecilia, Rome (fig. 5), with disarming directness and utter simplicity. Mochi's own contribution to the Capella Paolina, a travertine *Saint Matthew and the Angel*, is a response to his contemporaries' artistic aims, but, with its tendency toward complexity and its stunted figure, the work reveals his relative artistic immaturity. Still, the innovative spatial effects and concentrated force sought by Mariani and Maderno strongly affected Mochi's stylistic development.[6]

Mochi's breakthrough—a work that gave purpose and energy to these contemporary stylistic values—is the *Annunciation* in Orvieto (figs. 2–3). Commissioned by Mario Farnese, Mochi executed a sculptural group intended for the Cathedral in Orvieto. He finished the *Annunciate Angel* in 1605; three years later he returned to carve the companion figure, the *Virgin*. Each a superb work in its own right, the paired sculptures create an electrifying exchange. Spiraling downward, the angel is a cyclone of movement. Yet his gaze locks on the Virgin, and his left hand dramatically indicates the heavens, the source of the conception. By contrast, the *Virgin* is a compact, inwardly directed form. Her inner turmoil at the astonishing news borne by the angel is betrayed by the tautly pulled pleats of her robe, as she simultaneously shrinks from and is compelled toward the heavenly apparition. The brilliant conceit of her drapery caught between her chair and feet creates a graph of sharply diverging lines, which the sculptor extends through the whole composition to emphasize her anxiety and emotion. Mochi drew freely from artistic sources that impressed his generation; the *Virgin*'s silhouette may have been suggested by a statue from the Niobid group, a famous antique sculpture then in the garden of the Villa Medici in Rome; and the motif of tangled drapery at her feet possibly was suggested by Caravaggio's second painting of Saint Matthew (Rome, San Luigi dei Francesi, Contarelli Chapel).[7] But the sculptor subsumed these motifs within the clarity of Maderno's and Mariani's art and charged them with his own dynamic interpretation of Mannerist linearity to create a startlingly fresh image.

Preceding pages:

FIGURE 2. Francesco Mochi. *Virgin*, 1608. Marble; h. 210 cm. Orvieto, Opera del Duomo. Photo: Alinari/Art Resource, New York. The dynamic contrast between the *Virgin* and the *Annunciate Angel* (fig. 3) formerly in the interior of the Orvieto Cathedral attests to Mochi's remarkable sense of drama. The overwhelming impact of the angel's announcement is evident in the Virgin's tense posture and her anxious expression, and in the taut folds of her robe.

FIGURE 3. Francesco Mochi. *Annunciate Angel*, 1605. Marble; h. 185 cm. Orvieto, Opera del Duomo. Photo: Alinari/Art Resource, New York. Unlike Mochi's *Virgin* (fig. 2), the *Annunciate Angel* is seemingly in perpetual motion, gesturing dramatically toward heaven as he delivers his message.

FIGURE 4. Francesco Mochi. *Monument to Ranuccio Farnese*, 1612–20. Bronze; over-life-sized. Piacenza, Piazza Cavalli. Photo: Alinari/Art Resource, New York. The sweeping forms of this statue—creating the illusion of a horseman riding against the wind—give the *Monument to Ranuccio Farnese* an energy that distinguishes it from the more studied equestrian statues typical of the time. Of particular interest in this monument and its companion piece, the *Monument to Alessandro Farnese*, is Mochi's unusually vivid handling of the horse's mane and tail.

Mochi's ability to fuse line, movement, and mass into a single form is apparent in the masterworks of his career: the equestrian monuments in Piacenza and *Saint Veronica* in Saint Peter's Basilica in Rome. The bronze monuments to Alessandro (1545–1592) and Ranuccio (1569–1622) Farnese in Piacenza (see fig. 4) occupied much of Mochi's time from the first proposal in 1612 until the finishing touches to the second monument in 1629.[8] Equestrian statues have a long and distinguished history in Italy. By the beginning of the seventeenth century, however, Giovanni Bologna's statue of Cosimo I in Florence, unveiled in 1595, established a much-emulated formula that depended on a clear balance of proportions between rider and mount, and a sharp articulation of detail, all in an image of studied control. Mochi swept away these conventions in the statue of Ranuccio Farnese and even more so in the posthumous statue of his father Alessandro. Unlike the discrete elements of the Giovanni

Bologna type, Mochi's horse and rider (fig. 4) merge in a cadence of forms, the horse's mane blowing into the rider, whose robe flutters behind. Ranuccio seems to challenge the elements, as if unheedingly facing into a storm. This device energizes the composition, sending all movable parts into motion and creating a stirring image of a ruler challenging and triumphing over nature.

The long years required to finish the Piacenza statues resulted in fundamental works of the Baroque era. But by the time that Mochi returned to Rome, the artistic situation in the capital had changed. Bernini now controlled the city's sculptural projects politically and stylistically. Commissions of vast public monuments compelled him to organize workshops that employed many of the city's sculptors; this situation, in turn, reinforced a tendency to emulate Bernini's dramatic manipulation of mass and naturalistic detail. Mochi's linear and abstract vision, so powerful and original when introduced in the formative years of the Baroque, no longer synchronized with prevailing Roman Baroque taste. His dilemma is nowhere more evident than in the context of his *Saint Veronica* (fig. 6), one of the four colossal marbles that Bernini supervised as part of a program celebrating holy relics housed in the Crossing of Saint Peter's. The acute diagonal direction of the pleats of Saint Veronica's dress powerfully convey the saint's excitement at the discovery of Christ's image on her veil. To announce the miracle, she appears to hurtle out of her niche into the viewer's space. All of Mochi's talents serve to invigorate this statue and to carry its message across the cavernous interior of the basilica. Of the four sculptures that completed this program, only Bernini's *Saint Longinus* matched the force of Mochi's *Saint Veronica*.[9] Longinus's directional signals are implied in gestures rather than blatantly scribed, as in Veronica's long pleats. Bernini's swirl of powerfully massed and modeled drapery enveloping the Roman centurion clearly announced the future stylistic direction of Roman art, while Mochi's energetic linearism trailed away from the major artistic movement.

Disillusioned and frustrated by stylistic change and his increasing artistic isolation, Mochi turned in an unexpected direction, as much against the tide of taste as his early work. His late sculptures, like the *Baptism of Christ* (fig. 16), are spindly and ascetic, almost Gothic in their backward-looking artistic stance, but in fact they return to the pure abstraction of some early aspects of Mannerism. In a sense this late style does not represent a major deviation, as Irving Lavin has argued, as much as a deepening dematerialization of form and an internaliza-

tion of emotion already evident in his art.[10] Mochi was not alone in his rejection of the reigning artistic sensibility. Even if their forms differed from Mochi's, painters Guercino and Guido Reni also left Rome and turned to an otherworldly idealism in their late works.[11] Mochi's difficult and problematic career ended out of tune with the Baroque. Nonetheless, Mochi created a body of work that was filled with potential and reveals the creative forces that collided to form the Baroque style.

Mochi's Style

The identification of the *Bust of a Youth* as Mochi's work allows us to enumerate and celebrate those aspects of Mochi's style that helped to create the Baroque era. Since the work is as yet undocumented, its attribution rests on compelling visual comparisons with his known statues. A close analysis of the distinctive features of face, drapery, and particularly hair reveals those essential preoccupations that characterize Mochi's art. A close reading of the marble bust will also elucidate the differences between

FIGURE 5. Stefano Maderno (Italian, 1567–1611). *Saint Cecilia*, 1600. Marble; life-sized. Rome, Santa Cecilia. Photo: Alinari/Art Resource, New York.

FIGURE 6. Francesco Mochi. *Saint Veronica*, 1635–40. Marble; h. approx. 450 cm. Rome, Saint Peter's. Photo: Alinari/Art Resource, New York. Much of the dramatic effect of *Saint Veronica*, as in Mochi's *Virgin* and *Annunciate Angel* (figs. 2–3), lies in the artist's bold and distinctive linearism. This linear quality, which we can see most clearly in the diagonal folds of the saint's dress, contributes to the impression that Saint Veronica is moving toward the viewer.

FIGURE 7. Francesco Mochi. *Bust of a Youth* (alternate view of fig. 1). A comparison of this figure and the next reveals the similarity between the facial features of these two works. Comparisons of this sort have played an essential role in establishing that the bust is the work of Mochi.

Mochi, the artist to whom the sculpture is here attributed, and Bernini, to whom it was once ascribed.

Artists often create distinctive forms to represent human features, and these forms can become virtual signatures of style. That Mochi's work bears such idiosyncrasies is revealed in a comparison of the *Bust of a Youth* (fig. 7) with the *Annunciate Angel* in Orvieto (fig. 8). The youth and angel share the following characteristics: beneath a smooth, long nose, the lips part slightly, gently creasing the cheeks on either side. An indentation furrows the face above the lips, while a small pointed chin juts out below. The eyebrows are subtly defined, but the eyelids are bold and the pupils are each incised by perfect circles surrounding an iris gouged out at center. Cheekbones tightly stretch the smooth flesh. Above the fore-

head, the hair parts in the middle, frothing up like waves and cascading in swirling locks down either side. In the turning of the head, the neck muscle bulges tautly, while a curving crease of flesh separates neck from shoulder. While the bust's facial type is particularly analogous to this early work, it also bears a relation to such later sculptures as *Saint Veronica* (fig. 6). The shape of the lips, the small pointed chin, the wide open eyes, and the long nose of the *Bust of a Youth* are structurally similar to those of *Saint Veronica*, despite the more dramatic expression of the latter.

Drapery is the most notable aspect of Mochi's *Saint Veronica*: its crystalline pattern is a crucial element of the sculptor's style. Even the fraction of cloth cloaking the *Bust of a Youth*'s torso reveals the taut, almost mathe-

matical, system that characterizes his drapery style. On the *Bust of a Youth,* a sash slices across the tunic, tightly binding it against his chest and causing the pleats to gather and radiate from the pressure point. Veronica's drapery exhibits a similar concern with pattern: diagonal pleats converge at the upper right to guide the viewer's eye up to the veil. Compositionally, *Saint Veronica* contrasts parallel lines with circular patterns, such as the sleeve ringing Veronica's right arm or the folds trailing around her right leg. Similarly, the tight, angular pattern of the youth's garment is carefully determined and plays off the spiraling, apparently random, pattern of his hair. Within the precise linear frame formed by drapery and hair, the dreamy, longing look of the youth is startlingly apparent. The tension in the sharp pleats of the cloak thus serves to focus the subject's state of mind, just as the vivid pattern of Veronica's robe intensifies her excitement at the miraculous vision of Christ's face and the taut reverse twists of the Orvieto *Virgin*'s drapery reinforce her inner turmoil at the announcement that she will bear the son of God. Mochi was gifted in the use of drapery as a metaphor of emotion, and the *Bust of a Youth* is an accomplished example of his talents in this regard.

Nowhere does Mochi's inventive power and eccentric personality emerge more completely than in his treatment of hair. It is a natural substance subject to physical effects: ordinary hair can be tossed by the wind or shaken by the head; thick matted locks can be tousled by neglect; or carefully combed tresses can be neatly held by headbands. While the hair of Mochi's statues is convinc-

FIGURE 9. Francesco Mochi. *Bust of a Youth* (alternate view of fig. 1). Mochi poured much of his imaginative power into the sculpting of hair, as can be seen in this view of the back of the bust.

ingly real, it was nonetheless an aspect of the human figure that stimulated the artist's imagination. Mochi's hair reminds us of other artists' fascination with pattern and flow: Albrecht Dürer's renditions of knots or Leonardo's studies of water and storms were, similarly, exercises in finding order in what seems random or chaotic. The hair of Mochi's figures seems to have a structure like music, sometimes smoothly harmonious, sometimes wildly syncopated, but in each instance it is part of a carefully composed rhythm. Mochi's use of hair is also highly virtuosic: despite the intrinsic nature of marble or bronze, the artist convinces us that he has transformed intractable material into another matter.

The topmost locks of the *Bust of a Youth* curl away from a center like four ends of a ribbon tied into a bow and crinkled for decorative effect. As the locks fall from the head, they wind into tight corkscrews, framing the

face and weighing heavily on the shoulders. From the back (fig. 9), the hair seems to become increasingly random, but in patterns that respond to swirling forces like eddies of water or wind. These patterns become almost independent of the rest of the work. Isolating details of Mochi's hair on other statues, such as the tail of the horse carrying Ranuccio Farnese (fig. 4), reveals aspects that could stand on their own as objects of abstract beauty. Unidentified, the horse's tail looks like the frozen relic of an ice storm or the flickering of a flame. The artist successfully captured the ebb and flow of nature, but he imposed his own order on it. Seen as part of the monumental horse-and-rider, these strands of horsehair gather and organize the forces and momentum of the whole. The hair of the allegorical infants on the sides of the monument to Alessandro Farnese (see fig. 10) is more tightly controlled, each lock graven with double or triple ridges. These same precise lines and curves characterize the hair of the *Bust of a Youth*. On both works, the tresses spill turbulently across the head, resembling waves whipped up by a storm. Even in the marble, Mochi's form is so sharp that it often appears metallic.

The motif of locks radiating from the top of the head and the knobby protuberances they form on the sides relate the *Bust of a Youth* to the Orvieto *Angel*. Yet the strands of hair are more precisely chiseled on the bust, an effect seen on such later works as the angels on the Farnese equestrian monuments. The treatment of the back of the *Youth*'s head is also similar to such later sculptures as the *Bust of Cardinal Antonio Barberini, the*

Younger (c. 1629; fig. 11); in both cases, the hair is flattened on the head at top but becomes more three-dimensional as it approaches the edges. On the front of the two busts, however, Mochi's conceptions differ radically: the cardinal's hair sweeps back in long, thick strands, not in curls like the youth's.[12] The organization of the hair seems tighter and more controlled in the *Bust of a Youth* than in the cardinal's bust or in the *Saint John the Baptist* in Dresden (fig. 15), which features similar spiral locks, but which is deliberately chaotic and unruly.

Stylistic considerations assist the process of dating the *Bust of a Youth*. The overall structure of face and the composition of hair most closely resemble those aspects of the earlier Orvieto *Angel* of 1605. Yet the sharper

FIGURE 10. Francesco Mochi. *Monument to Alessandro Farnese* (detail), 1621–29. Bronze. Piacenza, Piazza Cavalli. This figure and the next illustrate again the distinctive stylization of hair that is often a feature of Mochi's sculpture. The tighter ringlets of this allegorical infant, a detail of the base of the *Monument to Alessandro Farnese*, contrast with the larger, flowing curls of the *Bust of a Youth* (see fig. 9).

carving seems more characteristic of Mochi's later work without, however, sharing its increasingly free structure. For instance, similarly twisted locks of hair appear on the *Saint John the Baptist*, carved after 1629; and the broad drapery folds over the youth's left shoulder bear comparison with those on the adult Saint John's right thigh. The sharp parallel grooves of the sash are similar to those on the *Bust of Carlo Barberini*, sculpted around 1630.[13] The sharply turned head and the truncation of the torso relate to the *Bust of Ladislao D'Aquinio* in Santa Maria-sopra Minerva, Rome, dated by Irving Lavin to 1621, but later according to other authors.[14] Mochi's relatively small production and the lack of dated milestones in his career hinders a precise chronology of his works. With our present knowledge of his life, it is only possible to date the *Bust of a Youth* approximately around the year 1630.

If the attribution to Mochi appears secure, why did earlier scholars attribute the *Bust of a Youth* to Bernini? The bust was first published in 1917 as the work of Bernini;[15] it is notable that the *Bust of Cardinal Antonio Barberini* (fig. 11) was also formerly attributed to Bernini before Mochi was recognized as its author.[16] Comparing the *Bust of a Youth* to a Bernini work of roughly the same period—if we accept a dating of Mochi's *Youth* to around 1630—sheds light on essential differences between the two artists. Bernini's first *Bust of Cardinal Scipione Borghese* (c. 1632; fig. 12) is a sculpture that embodies many of the attributes contributing to Bernini's success, and is a work that the sculptor himself acknowledged as one of his finest. (An often cited example of Bernini's virtuosity is the story that he discovered a flaw in the marble in the late stages of carving, yet finished a second version in only a few days.)[17] Bernini brought the cardinal to life with many devices of optical illusion: the head turns to give a sense of motion, the lips part as if to

FIGURE 11. Francesco Mochi, *Bust of Cardinal Antonio Barberini, the Younger,* c. 1629. Marble on black marble socle; h. 83.2 cm. (without base). The Toledo Museum of Art, Purchased with funds from the Libbey Endowment, gift of Edward Drummond Libbey (65.176). By permission of The Toledo Museum of Art.

speak, the pupils are cunningly gouged out to represent glinting eyes, the face sags and folds with utmost fidelity to the appearance of real flesh, and the short cape has an impressionistic pattern across its surface that suggests cloth crinkling with movement. In all, there is a sense of emotional warmth and physical ease in total harmony that expresses the confidence of the sitter as much as that of the sculptor.

In contrast, the *Bust of a Youth* is tense and rigid, not relaxed. An air of intensity suffuses this image. Mochi, too, used optical illusions to good effect, as in the swirling locks of hair, and the shadow formed by the open mouth, but his illusions are tightly structured and calculated. Mochi's *Bust of Pompilio Zuccarini* (c. 1638; fig. 13) is a brilliant exercise in optical illusion, but the zigzags of his cloak are so dependent on abstract pattern that they undercut any sense of naturalism. His drapery reads as a carefully planned conception; Bernini's is no

less planned, but it appears unstudied and intuitive. Mochi's clearly demarcated structure leads to compositions that are closed and self-contained. Bernini's, in contrast, are outwardly directed: his forms often seem to continue beyond the edge of the sculpture to include the viewer in the space implied by the sculpture. As a consequence, Mochi's subjects appear introverted and distant by comparison with Bernini's outgoing creations. With the *Bust of Cardinal Scipione Borghese* (fig. 12) in particular, Bernini strove to establish a sense of informality that would make it as accessible as possible.

Mochi's sense of abstraction tends, instead, to separate his sculpture from its audience. The *Bust of a Youth*'s radiating drapery pleats or curving pattern of hair is fundamentally different from the optical effects Bernini designed to achieve a convincing naturalism. At the heart of Mochi's art is a rigorously geometric sensibility, which is essentially different from the unchecked freedom that

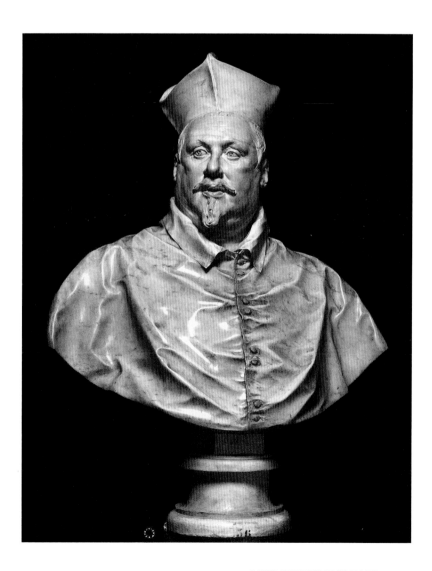

FIGURE 12. Gian Lorenzo Bernini (Italian, 1598–1680). *Bust of Cardinal Scipione Borghese,* c. 1632. Marble; h. 78 cm. Rome, Galleria Borghese. Photo: Alinari/Art Resource, New York. The astonishingly lifelike quality of Bernini's *Bust of Cardinal Scipione Borghese* — the first of Bernini's two busts of the cardinal — differs greatly from the more stylized quality of Mochi's *Bust of a Youth* (fig. 1).

FIGURE 13. Francesco Mochi. *Bust of Pompilio Zuccarini*, c. 1638. Marble; h. 70 cm (without base). Rome, Galleria Nazionale d'Arte Antica. In comparison with the animated *Bust of Scipione Borghese* by Bernini, Mochi's *Bust of Pompilio Zuccarini* has a studied and somewhat distant quality. The contrast between Bernini and Mochi is particularly noticeable in the differences between each sculptor's portrayal of fabric — the intricate pattern of lines and shapes in Zuccarini's cloak is quite different from the more naturalistic cape of Bernini's *Cardinal Scipione Borghese* (see fig. 12).

flows through Bernini's work. However difficult to execute, Bernini's sculptures make us believe that the physical task of making them was easy; the discipline of Mochi's works gives the impression of the painstaking attention required to bring each one to its level of focused clarity. While at first glance the *Bust of a Youth* may appear to exemplify Bernini's love of drama, movement, and bravura carving, with prolonged examination it becomes clear that the sculpture belongs to a different world, to Mochi's ideal realm of mathematical abstraction.

Mochi's Busts: Type, Subject, and Function

Busts are commonly associated with portraits of historical figures. Men and women have long wished to record their appearances for posterity, and the attraction of a sculpted portrait in materials like marble or bronze is that their durability guarantees the preservation of the sitter's features and the memory of his or her fame. Busts conventionally include the head and a portion of the torso. Generally, the portrait ends at the chest and does not include the arms. Accustomed to this format, the viewer accepts this fragment of the body. Sculptors have often had difficulties with the truncation of the body, however, seeking different solutions to slice the body horizontally or in a curve, and to disguise this line with drapery or to emphasize this concluding division. Mochi's *Bust of Cardinal Antonio Barberini* (fig. 11) is a good example of the Baroque bust, which tends to include a broad chest area to set off the head. The *Bust of a Youth* incorporates a smaller chest area into the composition; the proportion of head to chest is closer to the type preferred in the sixteenth century than later in the seventeenth century, possibly supporting an early dating in Mochi's career. However, the modest proportions are as appropriate to the youth's simplicity as the scale of the cardinal's bust is to that sitter's importance and dignity.

Just how free Mochi's approach to the form could be is evident in his *Bust of Pompilio Zuccarini* (fig. 13). The sculptor discarded structured depictions of robe and hair for an impressionistic carving of textures. The effect creates a blur of form around a harrowingly realistic portrait of the tired-looking canon of the church of Santa Maria ad Martyres (the Pantheon), where the work occupied a niche. As a strategy of presentation, it is the reverse of the *Bust of a Youth*, in which hair and robe are rendered with meticulous mimetic precision but the face is idealized to a state of perfection beyond the ordinary.

The question then arises, who (or what) is the subject of the Art Institute bust? It may portray an actual young man, but this is unlikely. Certainly contemporary artists like Caravaggio or Bernini painted and drew anonymous teenagers, captivated by their beauty and youth.[18] But marble was expensive, and busts carved from this material were usually commissioned by powerful and wealthy individuals like Antonio Barberini or Scipio Borghese, rather than by young unknowns. Furthermore, the youth's cloak appears to be ancient, not contemporary, and, as has been noted, his features are idealized, not particularized. Busts are not limited to important personages of the day, but can include mythological heroes, such as David, or revered religious subjects, such as Saint John the Baptist, and it is perhaps in this category that the bust belongs.

Tradition and the evidence of Mochi's career suggest that in this case the identity may be the young Saint John the Baptist, patron saint of Florence, where Mochi first trained. Saint John the Baptist was frequently depicted in central Italian paintings and sculpture. As a cult figure, John was represented at various ages, most often at the prime of life or as a youth, and both in full-length and bust form. Typically, he is shown wearing a rough garment, often of animal fur, which is held on with a strap, from which his baptizing cup can hang. Usually, his hair is tousled and unkempt from his life in the wilderness. Often he is characterized as gaunt and emaciated, but sometimes he is idealized, his look distant, as if in religious rapture. The *Bust of a Youth*'s gaze is not directed toward the world of the viewer but distinctly turned away, as if looking beyond this world. His distant look and transcendent expression are those of the seer longing for heaven.

A terracotta bust in the Art Institute dating from the mid-fifteenth century (fig. 14) displays the attributes and expression associated with this tradition: the rough garment held by a strap, the unruly hair, and the otherworldly gaze. While some Florentine busts of the young Saint John the Baptist, such as Antonio Rosselino's in the National Gallery of Art, Washington, D.C., show the youth with a fur shirt underneath a tunic, and a few depict him in a tunic without a rough garment, such as a work by the Master of David and Saint John statuettes in the Victoria and Albert Museum, London, Mochi's own late Baptist wears only a tunic, not a rough fur (fig. 15).[19] The absence of the fur shirt from the Art Institute marble prevents a certain identification, but does not preclude the subject of Saint John the Baptist.

Contemporary busts of religious figures place the *Bust of a Youth* in a typological context. Among the most popular and widely circulated was the pair of the young Christ and the Virgin produced in bronze by the Flemish sculptor Francesco Duquesnoy, who made his career in

FIGURE 14. Master of the Saint John Figures (circle of Donatello). *Saint John the Baptist*, c. 1470. Painted terracotta; h. approx. 49.5 cm. The Art Institute of Chicago, Gift of Mrs. Leopold Blumka, and Victoria and Anthony Blumka, in honor of John Maxon (1977.917). This bust is typical of traditional portrayals of Saint John the Baptist, who may be the subject of Mochi's *Bust of a Youth* (fig. 1).

Rome.[20] It is worth extending this comparison to note that Duquesnoy's bust type with the abbreviated chest is similar to that of Mochi's. Christ's pairing with his mother, as pendants, is also notable, since it is possible that the *Bust of a Youth* turned toward another figure; but the sharply twisted head was a favorite motif of Baroque sculptors, since it activated an artistic form that was inherently static. It is also possible that the bust was intended for a particular site and that its gaze was directed to a point in space, such as an altar.

Certainly Saint John the Baptist was a favorite theme of Mochi's, as well as of his principal patrons, the Bar-berini family. The sculptor named one of his sons Gio-vanni Battista, when he was born in 1628.[21] And a small marble of St. John the Baptist ("San Giovanni picolo di marmo"), possibly identical with the Art Institute bust, appears in an inventory of Mochi's possessions in his house on the Via Gregoriana compiled on March 13, 1654, a month after his death from fever.[22] This entry does not specify bust or head, nor whether it is by Mochi; but marble statuettes of the period are less common than busts and are not included among Mochi's known work. This inventoried work at least underscores his personal connection to the theme.

FIGURE 15. Francesco Mochi. *Saint John the Baptist*, c. 1629. Marble. Dresden, Hofkirche.

FIGURE 16. Francesco Mochi. *Baptism of Christ*, c. 1634. Marble. Rome, Museo di Roma, Palazzo Braschi. The austere figures in Mochi's *Baptism of Christ* establish a very different tone from that of the somewhat earlier *Bust of a Youth* (fig. 1). The comparative energy of the earlier sculpture has been replaced by the solemn and meditative approach of the *Baptism of Christ*, which is typical of Mochi's later work.

If the *Bust of a Youth* was not kept personally by the sculptor, then a likely patron for whom it was intended was Carlo Barberini. By June 1629, Barberini had commissioned Mochi to carve a statue of the adult *Saint John* (fig. 15), which, according to the biographer Giovanni Battista Passeri, was meant to replace Pietro Bernini's *Saint John* in the Barberini chapel in Sant'Andrea della Valle, Rome.[23] Passeri's story has been disputed by the scholar C. D'Onofrio, who pointed out that Mochi's adult *Saint John* could have been commissioned for the chapel of the baptismal font in the cathedral in Carlo's small fief Monterotondo, outside Rome.[24] But if Passeri's account is, after all, correct, perhaps the *Bust of a Youth* was intended for Monterotondo. Extensive records of this wealthy papal family survive, but these archives have yet to yield information about the bust.[25] The *Bust of a Youth* was owned early in the twentieth century by Gentile di Giuseppe, who collected Renaissance and Baroque art in Paris, and the bust remained in France after the dispersal of his collection.[26]

At the time of his death, Mochi was still at work on the *Baptism of Christ*, which remains unfinished (fig. 16). Commissioned by Orazio Falconieri for his family chapel in San Giovanni dei Fiorentino, Rome, possibly as early as 1634, the sculpture clearly reflects Mochi's late style and melancholy mood. It is profoundly meditative and, one senses, intensely personal. Stiff as tree trunks, the two men incline toward one another. Their painfully emaciated bodies leave no doubt of their utter conviction in the significance of their acts. The sculptor has carved their features with a severe realism to match their demeanor. The contrast with the *Bust of a Youth* could not be greater. The perfect, shining visage of the youth and the energy radiating from every inch of its surface reflect the heat of Mochi's art at full power and confidence, while the *Baptism of Christ* is deliberately awkward and drained of vitality. It is tempting to imagine these two images of John the Baptist together in Mochi's house at the end of his life, the small bust a reminder of the power of his full maturity and a reflection of the style that had startled Italy, the other a ghostly but moving relic of a creative talent.

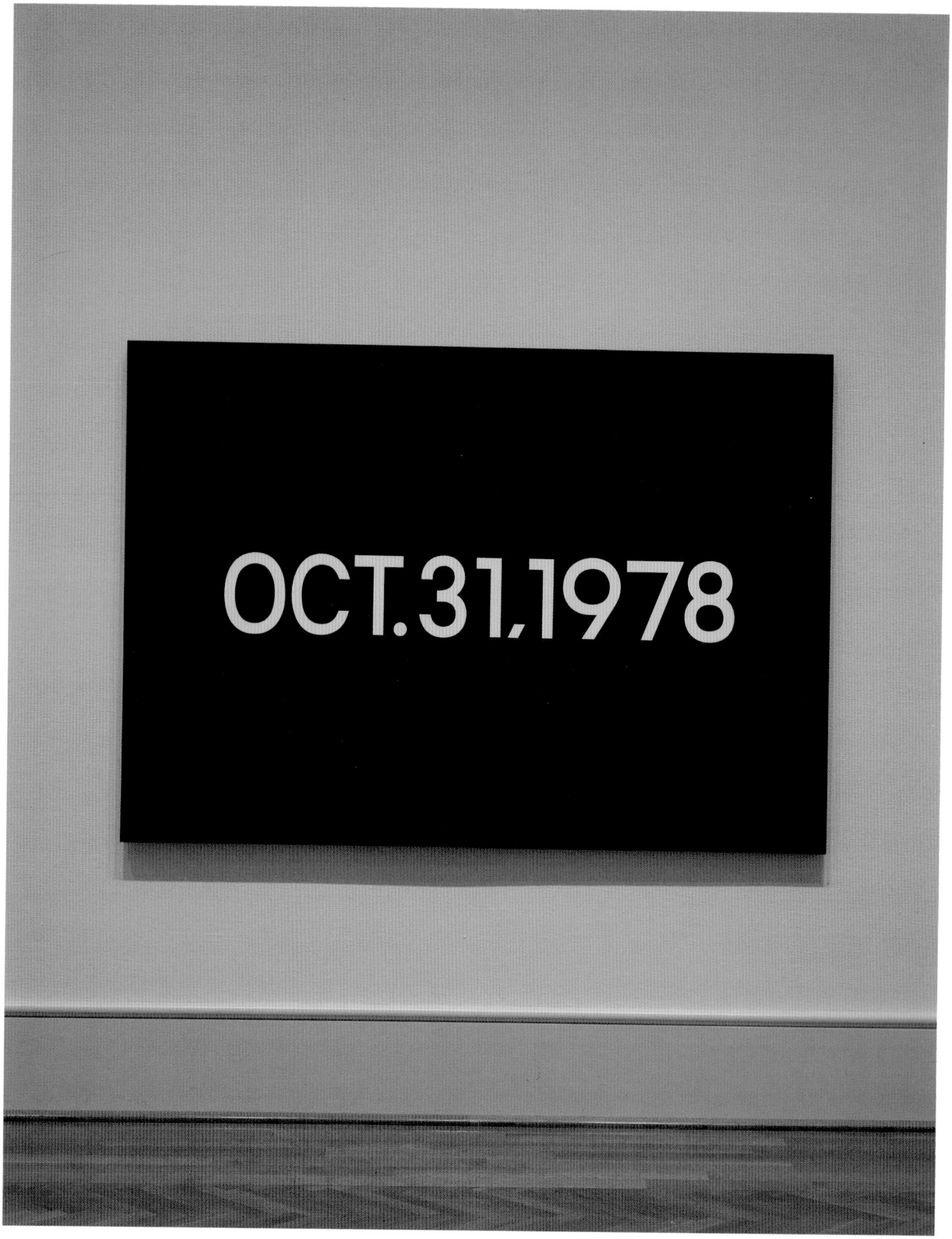
OCT.31,1978

The Date Paintings of On Kawara

ANNE RORIMER

Chicago

I have keenly experienced consciousness of myself today, at 81 years, exactly as I was conscious of myself at 5 or 6 years. Consciousness is motionless. And it is only because of its motionlessness that we are able to see the motion of that which we call time. If time passes, it is necessary that there should be something which remains static. And it is consciousness of self which is static.　　LEO TOLSTOI (1910)

Every life is many days, day after day. We walk through ourselves meeting robbers, ghosts, giants, old men, young men, wives, widows, brothers-in-love, but always meeting ourselves.　　JAMES JOYCE, *ULYSSES* (1922)

When On Kawara painted his first date painting on January 4, 1966, he inaugurated the *Today Series*, an ongoing, open-ended work now numbering more than 1,900 canvases. Many of these paintings have been exhibited in series as extensive as one year's production, and many have entered public and private collections either singly, in pairs, or in groups. In contrast to the other works that form part of Kawara's total oeuvre, the *Today Series* takes the form of traditional painting. While preserving the conventions of two-dimensionality, rectilinearity, and painted surface, *Oct. 31, 1978, Today Series ("Tuesday")* (fig. 1), acquired by the Art Institute in 1980, exemplifies the way in which Kawara has redefined traditional approaches to representional imagery.[1] Furthermore, it raises the question of its place within contemporary developments in painting and within the broader spectrum of the artist's aesthetic practice.

　　Each of Kawara's paintings represents a single day—the one designated by the actual date on which the work was made—and is considered by him to be a single component or detail of the *Today Series* as a whole. Letters, numerals, and punctuation marks, scaled to the size of the canvas, are placed laterally across its center. Although they give the impression of having been stenciled, the letters of the month, rendered in capitals and abbreviated when necessary, along with the numbers of the day and year, are skillfully drawn by hand in white upon a dark background. The typeface, subjectively chosen by the artist, subtly varies among paintings but is not determined by an objectively definable rationale or system. The earliest works in the series are a

FIGURE 1. On Kawara (Japanese, born 1933). *Oct. 31, 1978, Today Series ("Tuesday")*, 1978. Liquitex on canvas; 155.8 x 227.3 cm. The Art Institute of Chicago, Twentieth-Century Purchase Fund (1980.2). For the last twenty-five years, the Japanese conceptual artist On Kawara has undertaken a series of paintings, each of which records the date of its creation. Almost every day, Kawara embarks on a new painting, large or small in format, which he may or may not finish by the end of the day. If he does not finish the canvas in that day, it is destroyed.

cerulean blue, while others have been painted in red. For the most part, however, the background hues of the paintings tend to be dark gray-browns, gray-greens, or blues that verge on, but are never, black. Kawara applies four or five layers of paint to the background of each canvas and uses an additional six or seven layers of paint for the date. He obtains a rich matte surface but effaces all traces of the activity of brushwork.

Always horizontal in format, the *Today Series*, or so-called "date paintings," may be one of eight predetermined sizes, the smallest being 8 x 10 inches (20.3 x 25.4 centimeters) and the largest 61 x 89 inches (155.8 x 227.3 centimeters), like the one belonging to the Art Institute. Aside from the fact that a work must be started and completed on the actual day of its date, the artist does not impose a preconceived system of production. When they are small, as many as three paintings may be created in a day; on other days, none may be painted at all. If not finished by the close of the day, the partially completed painting is destroyed. Kawara, whose work has been exhibited extensively in the United States, Europe, and his own native country, Japan, and who has been based in New York City since the mid-sixties, travels extensively. Thus, works of the easily manageable sizes are more likely to be executed when the artist is away from home.

The significance of these paintings lies in the fact that they depict not only *a* date, but also their *own* date. If, historically, paintings have been fixed in time by a date on the front or back of the canvas, the date itself for Kawara becomes the subject of the painting and the sole embodiment of the work's figurative imagery. Each date painting, moreover, is unique if only by virtue of its particular date. Despite the fact that paintings of dates necessarily resemble each other, no combination of numerical or letter forms can ever be identical with another. Letters and numbers, which may be perceived as independent objects, allow an otherwise immaterial date to assume material form. The date paintings thus succeed in turning abstract, temporal measurement into the concrete reality of painting.

Because of their thematic involvement with temporality, the *Today Series* may tangentially be compared to the much earlier, nineteenth-century serial paintings of Claude Monet—to the fifteen *Haystacks* of 1890-91, for example

FIGURE 2. Installation view of eight paintings from a series of fifteen *Haystacks* that Claude Monet painted in 1890–91, shown in the exhibition "A Day in the Country: Impressionism and the French Landscape," on display at The Art Institute of Chicago in 1984–85. In addition to haystacks, Monet used a number of subjects for his series paintings, including poplars, cliffs, water lilies, and Rouen Cathedral. Within each series, Monet explored the effect of time on a scene in nature.

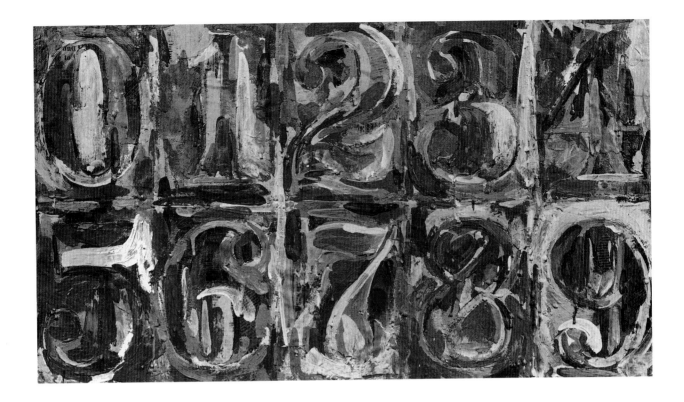

(see fig. 2). By working in series, Monet sought to capture the infinite, fleeting qualities of observed reality engendered by the ceaseless, but momentary, shifts in light—and, by extension, the passage of time—within the static format of multiple canvases. Kawara, quite differently, is not concerned with the specific effects of changing times on a given subject, as was Monet, but seeks instead to depict the notion of time itself.

The paintings of Kawara also may be viewed in comparison with the number and alphabet paintings of the mid to late 1950s by Jasper Johns (see fig. 3). For Johns, as for Kawara, the numeral or letter offered an already flat, abstract form as a subject for delineation, and, in the work of both artists, these symbols achieve a visual self-sufficiency. With regard to the work of Johns, as opposed to that of Kawara, the number or letter is absorbed into the dominant materiality of paint and brushwork. Johns subordinated numerical or lexical symbols to the demands of painterliness rather than to the demands of quantification or semantics. In canvases by Kawara, however, numbers and letters retain their informational purpose. If, for Johns, numbers and letters used as formal images primarily played a painterly role, for Kawara they maintain their symbolic function within the structure of a given date, as well as within the structure of the painted surface per se.

The *Today Series* reflects Kawara's understanding of the critical issues associated with painting that, as of the late 1950s and early 1960s, confronted artists internationally. The date paintings acknowledge and elaborate upon the significant ideas of artists such as Frank Stella or Robert Ryman in America, or Piero Manzoni in Europe, while they introduce original and unprecedented considerations of their own. At the end of the 1950s, in the wake of Abstract Expressionism and the School of Paris, a number of artists sought to revitalize painting, having found that the gestural handling of paint characteristic of the decade had been drained of its original power and

FIGURE 3. Jasper Johns (American, born 1930). *o through 9*, 1959. Encaustic and collage on canvas; 52 x 89 cm. Aachen, Neue Galerie, Sammlung Ludwig. Photo courtesy of the Leo Castelli Gallery, New York. In his number and alphabet paintings of the 1950s, Johns used a painterly style to represent abstract symbols. Much of the interest in Johns's *o through 9* lies in its bold brushwork; in contrast, Kawara's date paintings disguise the artist's hand, thereby emphasizing the informational aspect of the subject matter.

FIGURE 4. Frank Stella (American, born 1936). *Clinton Plaza*, 1959. Black enamel on canvas; 251 x 189 cm. Chicago, private collection. Kawara's date paintings are not unlike Stella's black paintings of the late 1950s and Robert Ryman's post-1957 paintings (see fig. 5) in their preoccupation with issues of representation. *Clinton Plaza* makes no clear reference to a reality outside the work itself, leaving the viewer to wonder about the role of illusion in art.

meaning. Speaking in general terms, it may be said that a number of artists on both sides of the Atlantic during this period sought to define a pictorial surface as something totally separate from any reality external to it. For this reason, these artists aimed to negate forms of expression overtly possessing emotional or transcendental overtones.

The question of how to make a painting that might exist as its own, nonreferential reality may be seen as the most crucial consideration of the years just prior to Kawara's first date painting. An often quoted statement of Frank Stella's is that in his paintings "only what can be seen is there," and that there is nothing there "besides the paint on the canvas."[2] This statement succinctly summarizes the goals of those artists desiring to remove personal and illusionistic references from painting. Stella's black paintings of 1958–60 (see fig. 4), for example, display neither figurative representation nor hierarchical compositional arrangement. They seek to conceal signs of the artist's intervention into the process of creation by eliminating the brushstroke with its tell-tale evidence of the artist's hand. Foreground and background merge in works that attempt to abolish illusionism of any kind.

Similarly, Robert Ryman took issue with earlier concepts of painting, maintaining as well that "what painting is, is exactly what people see."[3] Since 1957, he has devoted himself to paintings whose "image" is the paint surface itself once it has been applied to its support (see fig. 5). "There is never a question of what to paint," according to Ryman, "but only how to paint. The how of painting has always been the image—the end product."[4] Paintings by Ryman are purely self-referential in as much as they reflect only upon the activity behind their own painting. Canvases covered in white acrylic suggest the endless variation of surface texture brought about by the application of paint. In works by Ryman, this application is observed as being the visual end itself.

Before his death in 1963 at the age of thirty, Piero Manzoni had come to certain far-reaching conclusions, as his "Achrome" (meaning "no color") paintings attest. With the advent of his first Achrome in 1957, Manzoni began to realize the principles of his painting, later expressed in his 1960 text, "Free Dimension":

It is not a question of shaping things, nor of articulating messages. . . . For are not fantasising, abstraction and self-expression empty fictions? There is nothing to be said: there is only to be, to live.[5]

Rather than being painted, each Achrome simply came "to be." The first Achromes were made from canvas squares, which were soaked in the white, water-absorbant clay known as kaolin and then glued together side by side. When dry, the kaolin-soaked canvas became an earthy presence. Manzoni embraced a range of different materials—from cloth to fur to kaolin-covered bread rolls—in his quest for a "white surface that is simply a white surface

FIGURE 5. Robert Ryman (American, born 1930). *The Elliott Room: Charter V,* 1987. Acrylic on fiberglass with aluminum; 243 x 243 cm. The Art Institute of Chicago, Gift of Gerald S. Elliott (1990.132.5). Since the early 1960s, Robert Ryman has painted exclusively in white, exploring the subtlety of its hues and creating works that invite contemplative attention to the nature and texture of their painted surface.

and nothing else."[6] Although their means are as disparate as their results, artists like Stella, Ryman, and Manzoni have in common the basic motive of endowing painting with its own reality, exempt from any figurative, compositional, or psychological references.

Works in Kawara's *Today Series* dispense with illusionistic reference in a manner parallel to the paintings of these three artists. The letters and numbers of the day's date replace traditional imagery and composition. Instead, the placement and resulting "configuration" of abstract symbols lead naturally to "figuration," while the conventions of composition yield to the demands of "composing" the date. Kawara's paintings, like those of Stella, Ryman, or Manzoni, are self-sufficient and self-reflexive statements. The elements of each date serve as the curvilinear and linear parts of a coherent visual whole. In the sense that one cannot actually "see" a date, the paintings offer no information about their relationship to external reality, but within the confines of the painted canvas, the date—otherwise a mere abstraction—assumes a concrete form and shape. Within the very content of the work, therefore, the *Today Series* demonstrates how a painting can be a self-reliant presence, independent of (yet not disregarding) external points of reference. By virtue of existing as a date, each painting by Kawara asserts that *it* is "present," although paradoxically its date, perforce, refers to a time already past (see fig. 6).

The solid background hue of each date painting varies slightly from day to day and may change from gray to blue or, occasionally, to red so that the

FIGURE 6. Installation view of a date painting from the *Today Series* by On Kawara. Cincinnati Art Museum, RSM Company Collection. Photo: John Vinci. While Kawara's date paintings are self-referential in the sense that Stella's and Ryman's works are, they nevertheless do refer to an outside reality with their dates. The relation of the date paintings to the measurement and representation of time is powerfully suggested by this installation view from a business office, where Kawara's *Mar. 21, 1975* is surrounded by a calendar, a message pad, and other paraphernalia that are no doubt dated.

FIGURE 7. Ad Reinhardt (American, 1913–1967). *Abstract Painting # 11, 1961–66.* Oil on canvas; 152.4 x 152.4 cm. The Art Institute of Chicago, Gift of Dr. and Mrs. Irving Forman (1985.1067). For the last thirteen years of his life, Ad Reinhardt pushed his abstract art to new limits in black paintings that examined the means of distilling painting to its own essence within a field of monochromatic color. Reinhardt's approach to color has much in common with that of Kawara, who uses a uniform tone in each painting as he varies the color from work to work.

question arises as to what role color performs in these works. Stella's early black paintings, Ryman's white paintings, and Manzoni's "colorless" works similarly aim to avoid the representational, symbolic, or emotional associations that color can create. In the late 1950s, the issue of color was explicitly dealt with in contrasting manners by Ad Reinhardt in America and by Yves Klein in Europe. Their similar use of one hue bears comparison with the single background color of Kawara's date paintings, although in each instance their ultimate intentions differ.

Whereas Reinhardt after 1953 began to paint only with black in order to employ, like Manzoni, a "noncolor," Klein after 1957 turned to the almost exclusive use of the deep, electric cobalt blue now known as "International Klein Blue." With the desire to eradicate all extraneous and distracting visual elements from painting, Reinhardt sought the reduction of color to noncolor by pushing it to the edge of perception (see fig. 7). Klein operated in quite the opposite spirit, attempting to elevate color to mythical proportions while claiming that "through color, I experience a complete identification with space, I am truly free."[7] Reinhardt wrote that "there is something wrong, irresponsible and mindless about color, something impossible to control."[8] Klein, however, declared that "before the colored surface one finds oneself directly before the matter of the soul."[9] From opposite vantage points, both artists defined painting as a reality unto itself, with Reinhardt wishing to distill it to its own essence[10] and Klein believing that "paintings are living, autonomous presences."[11] Reinhardt viewed color as an interference in the expression of purity, while Klein considered it the means of envisioning an infinite and immaterial reality outside of "the psychological world of our inherited optics."[12]

FIGURE 8. On Kawara. Cardboard box and newspapers for *Oct. 31, 1978, Today Series ("Tuesday")* (see fig. 1). Photo: Anne Rorimer. In this figure and the next, we can see an expression of the particularity of each date on which Kawara paints. Each of the date paintings is accompanied by a newspaper (or, as in the case of fig. 9, a portion of a newspaper) from the day and place that Kawara painted the work.

Kawara's attitude toward color falls in between the opposing aesthetic positions of Reinhardt and Klein. In contrast to both, Kawara makes no claim for color in either a positive or negative way. He neither attempts to suppress it nor does he espouse a belief in its power to surpass mundane reality. Color, for Kawara, indicates the subtraction of light. The white lettering and colored background of the date paintings, alludes, in essence, to the contrast between the light of day and the dark of night.[13] While color lends definition to objects, it may also carry with it symbolic or emotional associations; but in Kawara's work, color does not carry such associations, and can be analyzed, finally, only in terms of saturation, value, or hue. Within its painted context, the color of each work is as unequivocal as its date, and no two paintings are exactly alike.

The question of how color might relate to the events of the day or to Kawara's state of mind—the question, that is, of why the artist chooses a certain color for a date painting—cannot be definitively answered. Whether a date painting is bright red or dark blue or one of many dark grays makes no thematic difference except for the fact of difference itself. Slight changes from one gray to another, as well as greater shifts from gray to blue or red, spare these works from any dogmatism. Rather, the background color of the date paintings, unspecified with regard to particular associations, allows for infinite diversity. A red or blue is as meaningful as one of the many varied tones of gray found in the majority of date paintings.

By imposing limits but not restrictions on his choice of color, Kawara establishes an endless potential for nuance. The unlimited variation of color means that the artist's choice of shade or hue loses its explicit meaning. Subjectivity and objectivity of selection cancel out each other, for the subtle differentiation in color leads to the appearance of sameness while simultaneously disproving it. Because pigmentation is an element of perception that "colors" whatever is seen in an inexplicable but multifaceted manner, the color of each date painting, like its date, may elicit certain thoughts but remains a quality unto itself without referring to particular ideas or feelings. The indeterminable degree to which physiological and psychological factors play a part in human vision thus enhances the dual sense of factual immediacy and impenetrable mystery manifested by these works.

Kawara's date paintings are based on a reality experienced as the temporal segments that record the continuous change from night to day and vice versa. Each work possesses a subtitle and, also, is accompanied either by a hand-made cardboard box that contains a newspaper of that day from the city where the work was painted (see fig. 8), or by a portion of a newspaper page that is glued to the inside lid of the box (see fig. 9). The subtitles range in content from long quotations to short phrases, from a notation of a personal thought to an international event. In recent years, they merely have stated the day of the week. The box affirms the painting's definition as an object in its own right, while the subtitles and newspaper anchor the work of art to — while juxtaposing it with — the existing, daily reality.

The inclusion of a newspaper or section of a newspaper in the box belonging to each painting accentuates the dichotomy between art and everyday actuality while simultaneously linking them together. The fact that the

FIGURE 9. On Kawara. *Dec. 17, 1979, Today Series ("Monday")* (with cardboard box and newspaper), 1979. Liquitex on canvas; 46.2 x 61.7 cm. New York, The Museum of Modern Art, Blanchette Rockefeller Fund. As this figure shows, a date painting may be displayed in conjunction with its accompanying newspaper and box.

FIGURE 10. Pablo Picasso (Spanish, 1881–1973).
Bottle of Vieux Marc, Glass, Newspaper, 1913.
Charcoal and pasted papers; 62.6 x 46.9 cm.
Paris, Le Musée national d'art moderne.
Kawara's use of newspapers has a distinguished
lineage: Picasso drew inspiration from them
during the early part of the century, and Andy
Warhol (see fig. 11) used them in the 1960s to
comment ironically on the pervasiveness of
mass-produced images.

boxed newspaper may or may not be exhibited with its painting emphasizes
the independence and interdependence of the two. Since the early part of this
century, when Georges Braque and Pablo Picasso introduced newsprint into
their collages (*papiers collés*), the daily newspaper has acted as a representa-
tive from the nonart, material world, as distinct from the fictional world of
the painted canvas or drawing. In *Bottle of Vieux Marc, Glass, Newspaper* of
1913 (fig. 10), Picasso, interestingly enough, curtailed the word "Journal"
(newspaper) to "Jour" (day), perhaps as an "in" joke within the work, since
the penciled bottle of marc is "vieux" (old) while the newsprint pertains to
that day. In contradistinction to the artists of Cubist collage, who integrated
newspaper fragments into an overall pictorial fabric, Kawara deliberately
keeps the newpaper physically separate from the painting. Metaphorically
drawing a distinct line between the reality of art and nonart, Kawara nonetheless refers to their "real," if intangible, connection. Painting and newspaper are thus cross-referenced by Kawara without being literally grafted
together.

The newspaper accompanying the date paintings grounds them in the
world of constant flux and continuing events (as opposed to the supposed
"timeless" context of art). In this regard, one is reminded of paintings by
Andy Warhol of the early 1960s that depict front-page headlines from tab-

loids or newspapers (see fig. 11). In Warhol's case, the newspaper provided already existing mass-produced, gripping, nonart imagery with an emphasis on shock-value. For Kawara, the newspaper is not subject matter for direct translation into painting as it is for Warhol, but rather is a temporal gauge of ongoing, *daily* reality. The newspaper is part of a date painting in its entirety, but remains in its own nonart domain at the same time, thereby providing a link to those phenomena—however down-to-earth yet ungraspable they may be—that, available to all, transpire from day to day. In addition, the conjunction of newpaper and date painting substitutes for the artist's hand-written signature an "authoritative" mark of validation based on real, if sensational, occurences.

Transitional works by Kawara of the early 1960s suggest artistic interests that would culminate in the date paintings. A work entitled *Nothing, Something, Everything* (fig. 12), for example—one of hundreds of drawings of this period—anticipates the *Today Series* in various ways. Black, Letraset, capital letters form the word "something." A pencil line encloses the letters within a rectangular perimeter that follows the shape of the paper. The word "some-

FIGURE 11. Andy Warhol (American, 1928–1987). *A Boy for Meg,* 1962. Synthetic polymer on canvas; 182.9 x 132 cm. Washington, D.C., National Gallery of Art (1971.87.11). Photo courtesy of the Leo Castelli Gallery, New York.

thing" is singled out, isolated, aggrandized. As the subject of pictorial representation, it stands alone and demands consideration as to exactly what it might stand for: a quantity or an object? For how much or what? Literally out of context and therefore providing no supporting verbal information, the letters of *Nothing, Something, Everything* assume a visual form. Set within the outline of the traditional rectangular format, they come to be "read" as shapes. The word, therefore, becomes the subject of the picture as both a two-dimensional object and as an abstract signifier.

A drawing entitled *Egg* (1964), whose capital letters, outlined in pencil, nearly fill a rectangular penciled boundary, and a 1964 drawing called *Rulers*, depicting two suspended yardsticks, similarly set the stage for Kawara's major work to come. The three letters spelling "egg" proclaim their independence as visual elements that still partake in the creation of verbal meaning. *Rulers* subtly confronts the question of perspective and illusion. The yardsticks, drawn in pencil, appear to hang at different distances from the spectator, in the space of a sketchily implied room, because the left-hand ruler, appearing closer, is longer than the right-hand one. By having drawn tools, which in practical life convey precise information about reality, Kawara points to the paradoxical nature of two-dimensional representation. In this drawing the two rulers have significance solely as pictorial elements, and not as useful implements that register distance factually. As such, they "rule out," so to speak, the false rendition of three-dimensional space by revealing its fictitious nature. In these early works, image and language merge as "something" or "egg" on the pictorial plane, which, as *Rulers* reminds us, remains

FIGURE 12. On Kawara. *Nothing, Something, Everything*, 1963. Letraset and pencil on paper; 20.5 x 30.5 cm. Photo courtesy of the artist. Early in his career, Kawara began to use language as a subject for his drawings and other works. The word "something" here exists outside a clear verbal context, and therefore assumes a compelling visual dimension.

flat despite its potential ability to deceive. Having rejected the use of illusion-istic devices, these drawings foreshadow the literal and factual quality of the ensuing date paintings.

Other works preceding the date paintings, such as *Questions: "Give Sentences..."* (fig. 13) and *Code* (1965), lend further insight into Kawara's artistic method. The former work presents two columns of different idioms, handwritten within a square, using the verb "to take" as a point of departure for phrases such as to take off, to take out, to take part in, etc. Written above the two columns is the directive, "Give sentences with the following." Provided with the building blocks for producing endless sentences, the viewer nonetheless has access only to what is visibly there, to the pattern made by the handwritten words. The latter work, *Code,* translates the text of a narra-tive into horizontal lines comprised of colored markings. Resembling a kind of generic script, they forfeit their original verbal content. Even if a computer were to break the code by translating the colors determined by the artist into words, the answer to the question, inherent in this piece, as to what distin-guishes one form of meaning from another—the verbal or the visual—would not ultimately be answered. Evolving from works such as these, the date

FIGURE 13. On Kawara. *Questions: "Give Sentences...,"* 1964. Pencil on paper; 35.5 x 43 cm. Photo courtesy of the artist. Kawara's understanding of the visual patterning of words is evident in this early work, where the myriad possibilities for sentences with the verb "to take" are listed matter-of-factly.

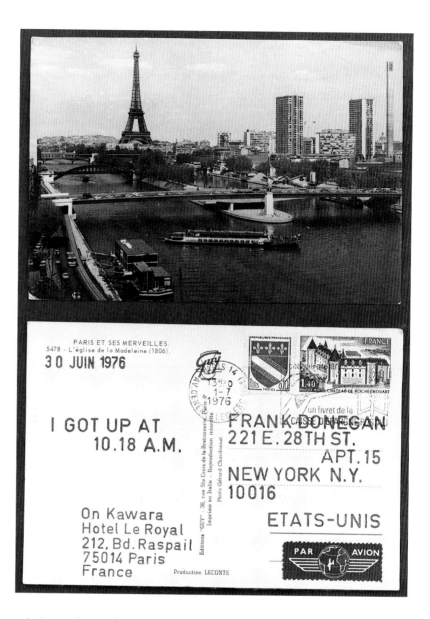

FIGURE 14. On Kawara. *I Got Up at 10.18 A.M.,* 1976. Rubber-stamped ink on postcard. Photo courtesy of the artist. For eleven years, Kawara sent a series of postcards to selected people announcing when he began each day. Each of Kawara's postcards and telegrams (see fig. 15) marked clearly the date and place of its origin, and functioned as part of an ongoing series.

paintings rely on the components of written communication in order to make their particular visual statement.

Paintings by Kawara, with their stark and striking presentation of the date on which each was created, point to the moment of their genesis and thus demarcate their own place within the span of history. If, on one level, a date is mute as an image, on another level it stands for the infinite number of events—from the most personal to the most universal—that "take place" on specific dates. Like temporal signposts, the date paintings emblematically punctuate their environment, whether they are inserted into the midst of other works of art or isolated on a wall by themselves.

By means of his art, Kawara brings time—which may be thought of as the major organizational force behind human experience and consciousness—into tangible, representational view. In addition to the *Today Series,* Kawara's activity as an artist encompasses a number of other significant, ongoing works that similarly seek to position themselves—and by extension, the viewer—with reference to his own, ultimately finite lifespan, invisibly set against the background of spatial and temporal infinity. Since 1966, in tandem with the introduction of the date paintings, Kawara has maintained a series of loose-leaf notebooks that comprise a work entitled *I Read*. Sequential pages, correlated with each day of the year on which he has made a painting, contain clippings from the daily press, which Kawara glues on a single, standard sheet of ordinary graph paper stamped with the day, month, and year. The early clippings for *I Read* provided Kawara with the subtitles for the paintings of that particular day and, in this way, initially inspired the idea for this work. Additionally, the clippings are taken from newspapers published in the place where the date painting was done.

Furthermore, each day since 1968 Kawara has kept a similar series of notebooks to form the work *I Went*, as well as a work in the same notebook format called *I Met*. The former group of notebook volumes contains a record of the artist's itinerary that he marks in red ink on a xeroxed map of the city where he happens to be. Documenting his daily course along city streets, Kawara translates his movement from one destination to another (necessitated by errands, sightseeing, or the normal demands of life in general) into the planar linearity of drawing. The latter set of volumes consist of individual pages, also stamped with the date, on which Kawara has typed the name(s) of anyone known to him whom he might have encountered throughout the twenty-four hour period. In this work, language, in place of line, reveals those points of interpersonal contact that connect over time to form a social framework for individual existence. Kept together by the artist, these three works (*I Read, I Went,* and *I Met*) bring abstract time into view vis-à-vis the concrete reality of people, places, or events by utilizing available systems of representation—the news media, maps, or proper names—to formally convey their content.

Kawara also takes advantage of existing modes of communication to deliver, quite literally, his aesthetic message. From 1968 until 1979, he consistently mailed a series of postcards, one per day, to two selected people. In

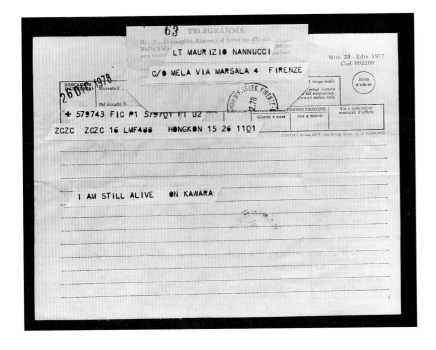

FIGURE 15. On Kawara. *I Am Still Alive,* 1978. Telegram. Photo courtesy of the artist.

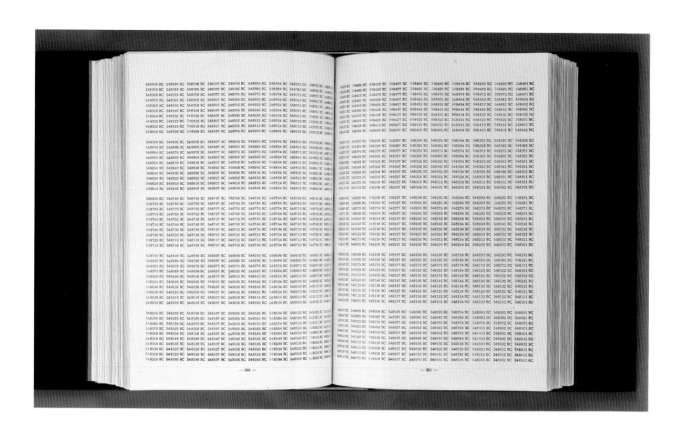

every case, the cards present a typical, horizontal scene from, or overview of, the place where Kawara was living or visiting at the time (see fig. 14). The recipient of a card would thus be informed as to the artist's geographical whereabouts by means of a pictorial short-hand image from a particular location. On the other side of the card, Kawara stamped the time, to the exact minute, at which he started the day, prefaced by "I got up at." The custom of sending postcards, in essence, provided him with a method for questioning the "timelessness" of art, allowing him instead to emphasize its potential as a vehicle for communication and representation over its (market) value as a permanent, precious object.[14]

Telegrams (and, more recently, Mailgrams), which Kawara has sent intermittently since 1970 to selected recipients, likewise rely on modern-day modes of communication (see fig. 15). The urgent message from the artist reads, "I am still alive," reminding the receiver of the brevity of individual existence. Kawara demonstrates, as well, the fact that a work of art need not be restricted to traditional representational forms, or exist as a singular and unique object, or be acquired through the commercial channels of buying and selling.

Two works, *One Million Years—Past* (fig. 16) and *One Million Years—Future* (fig. 17), convey the vast, yet measurable, expanse of time from 998031 B.C. through A.D. 1969 and from A.D. 1981 through 1001980.[15] Nine rows of sequentially typed columns of individual years, separated by decade, cover the white, 8½ x 11-inch pages that are contained within the two sets of notebooks, numbering ten volumes apiece. By representing the last one million years and the next million to follow within the real space of a book or, more precisely, within a "volume," in the double sense of the word, Kawara imbues the otherwise immaterial concept of time with concrete materiality. As in all of his works, numbers and letters fuse their symbolic, representational purpose with their function as visual shapes. In this way, Kawara integrates physical form with thematic content in the realization of works that illustrate the human capacity to grasp time and space in abstract, visible terms.

FIGURE 16. On Kawara. Pages from *One Million Years—Past*, 1969. Photo courtesy of the artist. This work and its companion piece, *One Million Years—Future* (fig. 17), visualize a vast expanse of time in the concrete terms of numerical representation, here contained within these massive volumes.

FIGURE 17. On Kawara. *One Million Years—Future*, 1981. Photo courtesy of the artist.

Chagall's *White Crucifixion*

ZIVA AMISHAI-MAISELS

Hebrew University, Jerusalem

In 1938, Marc Chagall executed the first of a series of major crucifixion paintings, the *White Crucifixion* (fig. 1), in which he combined traditional and new iconographical elements to provide the subject with a novel meaning. This painting, as well as those that followed, has been the center of a great deal of controversy, as various theorists have pondered the problem of why a Jew renowned for his treatment of Jewish themes began at this time to turn persistently to such a pronouncedly Christian subject.[1] This article will examine the painting within the religious, political, and personal context in which it was painted, taking into consideration the origins of the theme in Chagall's work, his statements on the subject, and his later development of it.

In the *White Crucifixion*, Christ is depicted wearing a short headcloth rather than a crown of thorns, and a fringed garment in lieu of the traditional loincloth. This garment is a variant on the Jewish ritual prayer shawl: it has two black stripes near its fringed edge and longer fringes in the corners. Above Christ's head, just over the limits of the upper bar of his T-shaped cross, appears the traditional INRI sign ("Jesus of Nazareth King of the Jews"), which is translated on the cross-bar itself into Aramaic: *Yeshu HaNotzri Malcha D'Yehudai*. This inscription, like the fringed garment, is used to stress Jesus's Jewish character, as Aramaic is written in Hebrew characters and was a language spoken by many Jews in Jesus's time. Chagall's spelling of the Aramaic allowed him a play on words, for the term "HaNotzri" is more usually used to mean "the Christian" than either "the Nazarene" or "the man from Nazareth." He thus emphasized Jesus's importance to both Christians and Jews, for the Jewish Jesus with his covered head and fringed garment is also a Christian.

Chagall further stressed this duality in his illumination of the scene: Christ is lit by a ray of white light from on high, but the Christian halo around his head is balanced at his feet by the halo surrounding the menorah, one of the oldest symbols of Judaism. This Jewish context is echoed above in four figures—three biblical patriarchs and a matriarch—who are dressed in explicitly Jewish garments: the man in white wears phylacteries and a prayer shawl, while the others cover their heads either with a skullcap, a mantle, or a kerchief. They hover above the cross to mourn Christ's death, floating out of the darkness into the ray of light that illuminates him.

This combination of Christian and Jewish motifs would have been complicated enough, but Chagall added to their complexity by placing the historical Jesus in a modern setting. The artist painted smaller, "explanatory" scenes around the crucified figure like those in a Russian icon, but he integrated them into the landscape, so that it seems that both they and Christ inhabit the same time and space.[2] To Christ's left (on the right side of the painting), Chagall depicted a synagogue, whose Torah ark goes up in flames, while a booted soldier with baggy trousers, who may be responsible for the fire, opens its doors to

FIGURE 1. Marc Chagall (French [born Russia], 1887–1985). *White Crucifixion*, 1938. Oil on canvas (with details painted over at a later date); 155 x 139.7 cm. The Art Institute of Chicago, Gift of Alfred S. Alschuler (1946.925). Chagall's use of Christian imagery within works devoted primarily to Jewish life has mystified many observers. The imagery of the *White Crucifixion* was originally designed to draw the attention of the Christian world to the dire plight of Jews in Nazi Germany. Within a very short time of finishing the work, however, Chagall painted over some of its details, obscuring the more obvious references to the Nazis, perhaps out of fear of prosecution (see figs. 2–4).

reveal the scrolls within. Below the soldier lie other objects from the pillaged synagogue: an overturned chair, the torn remnants of a prayer book, a Hanukah menorah with a tall backstand, and what appears to be a lamp, perhaps the Eternal Light that once hung before the ark. Further below, but still part of the same scene, an open prayer book and a smoking Torah scroll lie violated on the ground. The fire and the scattered objects document the pogrom that has taken place in the synagogue. It is from this scene of destruction that the Wandering Jew attempts to escape to the right, carrying his sack on his back. Below him, a mother shields her baby as she too runs away, this time toward the bottom of the painting. This scene continues on the other side of the cross, where three more bearded Jews escape toward the bottom left. One wipes away his tears as he flees; another, in torn garments, wears an unreadable sign on his chest; while the third, who looks back in horror at the burning synagogue, escapes wearing only one shoe, but clutching a Torah scroll in his arms, successfully saving it from destruction.

This pogrom has been visited not only on a synagogue, but also on an entire village. Above these three refugees, houses lie overturned, broken open, or burning in the snow. To the left, a Jew, seemingly consumed by the flames, lies dead and unburied amid the tombstones of the cemetery. Above him stands his empty chair, attended by his faithful goat, who appears to wait for him to return to it. Other former inhabitants of the village sit outdoors on the snow-covered ground amid the destruction, with a basket and a fiddle beside them, too dispirited either to eat or to console themselves with music. In front of them, other dispossessed inhabitants of the town try to flee in an overloaded boat, but since it has only one oar, it seems stuck in the white waters, unable to move. Despairing, the refugees lean over the side of the boat, trying to figure out a way to get it to move, or raise their hands to the heavens or to Jesus, seeking salvation. Above the village, a crowd of peasants enters, waving red flags and carrying swords and farm implements as weapons. They resemble the fleeing villagers, and it is at first not clear whether they are the perpetrators of the pogrom or the defenders of the village. In the latter case, their meager weapons seem inadequate to effect the hoped-for salvation.

To understand this painting, one must be aware that it is clearly dated 1938 at the lower right, and yet when it was first published in 1939 and exhibited in 1940, Chagall dated it 1939 on both occasions. This suggests that the work was completed in the last third of 1938 because Chagall constantly assigned works painted after his return from summer vacation in September to the following year, conforming to the Jewish rather than the Christian New Year.[3] On the other hand, the date on the painting itself suggests that, in the artist's mind, the work is indisputably connected with events of 1938.

Moreover, the painting is currently not in its original form, for Chagall overpainted some of the details that helped to pinpoint its meaning more exactly. These details are visible in a reproduction published in *Cahiers d'art* (fig. 2) in the second half of 1939, before the painting was exhibited. First of all, the sign worn by the Jew on the left bore the clearly legible German inscription: *Ich bin Jude* ("I am a Jew") (fig. 3). Second, both the flag above the burning ark and the armband of the soldier who has just opened its doors bore an inverted swastika (fig. 4), as though Chagall was loathe to draw this feared symbol correctly and, therefore, superstitiously reversed it. These details are repeated in a sketch of the painting (fig. 5) probably executed at the time Chagall made the changes, in order to keep his own record of its original state. The drawing elaborates on the original painting by suggesting that the books lying on the ground in front of the ark are the remnants of a book-burning scene, a detail not evident in the original painting.[4]

Whereas Chagall explained to Franz Meyer that he had altered the painting "because he found its statement too 'literal,'"[5] just when he made the changes is not clear. They may have been made before he exhibited the work in Paris in late January 1940, after the start of World War II, because he was unsure how the French would react to such obvious political elements in his work. The photograph of this exhibition published in *Cahiers d'art* (fig. 6) is not clear enough to be used as evidence: the configurations on the flag and the sign can be read as indicating either their original or their revised forms.[6] The changes, however, could also have been made either after Germany's invasion of France in May 1940, or after its defeat in June, because such clear symbols would have endangered the painting's safety if it had fallen into Nazi hands.[7] Another possible date for the changes—again to safeguard it—would be April 1941, when Chagall crated the painting for shipment via Lisbon to New York. The need for such precautions is amply demonstrated by two facts: first, that Chagall was arrested and detained for a while by the Germans in Marseilles as he tried to get to Lisbon; and, second, that the crated paintings were impounded by the German embassy in Madrid en route to Lisbon and by the Spanish authorities in Lisbon, arriving in New York only through the help of Chagall's daughter Ida.[8] In any event, it is clear that the changes had been made by

FIGURE 2. Marc Chagall. *White Crucifixion* (original state). Photo: *Cahiers d'art* 14, 5–10 (1939), p. 152. The details that Chagall later painted over (see figs. 3–4) are apparent in this reproduction of a photograph taken before the *White Crucifixion* was displayed publicly.

FIGURE 3. Marc Chagall. *White Crucifixion* (original state; detail of fig. 2). Photo: *Cahiers d'art* 14, 5–10 (1939), p. 152. This detail of the painting's original state reveals that the sign worn by the man in the lower left corner bore a message: *Ich bin Jude* ("I am a Jew").

May 1944, at which time a photograph of the work was published in *Liturgical Arts*.[9] It is also evident that the changes were not meant to be temporary: Chagall did not repaint the details upon arrival in New York or after its appearance in *Liturgical Arts*, although the painting was in his possession for most of the time until its exhibition at The Museum of Modern Art, New York, in 1946.[10]

Whenever these changes were made, the original details of the painting and the drawing (figs. 3–5) prove that the subsidiary scenes around Christ were meant to be depictions of actual events in Nazi Germany to which Chagall was reacting. Thus, the book-burning and the labeling of Jews with such a sign were common practices.[11] The latter may also refer to the first Jewish census (May 17, 1938), the registration and marking of Jewish businesses (June 14, 1938), the forced adoption by Jews of the names Abraham and Sarah (August 17, 1938), and the stamping of the letter "J" ("Jude") into Jewish passports (October 5, 1938)—all events that happened while Chagall was working on the painting.[12] Moreover, the burning of the Torah ark and the desecration of the scrolls in

the *White Crucifixion* were clearly inspired by the destruction of the synagogues in Munich and Nuremberg on June 9 and August 10, 1938, while the pogrom on the left side of the painting can be linked with those that occurred throughout the year, reaching their height on *Kristallnacht* (Crystal Night, November 9–10, 1938). The attempts of Jews during the 1930s to emigrate from Nazi Germany is represented in the painting by the Jews who try to escape the destruction. Their flight in all directions derives from a Yiddish poem by Abraham Walt that Chagall had illustrated shortly before. Walt asserted that the patriarch Jacob had thought of a plan that has saved the Jews to this day: if threatened, the Jews scatter, so that if one is killed, the others will be saved.[13] Even the armed peasants at the upper left have historical meaning, as their red flags indicate that they are Russian Communists. They should thus not be read as attacking the village but as coming to relieve it, for, in 1938, Russia was in the vanguard of resistance to Nazi plans for the domination of Europe. Chagall, like many others at this time, believed that liberation from the Nazi yoke could be

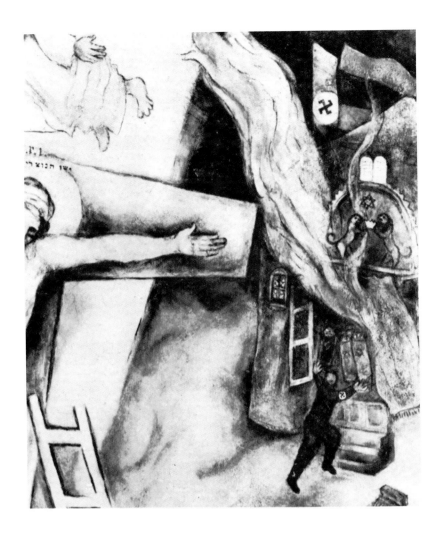

FIGURE 4. Marc Chagall. *White Crucifixion* (original state; detail of fig. 2). Photo: *Cahiers d'art* 14, 5–10 (1939), p. 152. In this detail of the original state of the *White Crucifixion*, we find other details that Chagall later obscured: inverted swastikas on a flag and on the armband of a soldier. Chagall's placement of inverted swastikas near the burning Torah ark and the desecrated synagogue demonstrate conclusively that, in the *White Crucifixion*, Chagall's cry against anti-Semitism was tied to contemporary events in Nazi Germany.

achieved with Russian aid, although he made it clear here that the Russians were not yet able to combat the evil and may arrive too late to help.[14]

Thus, the scenes surrounding Christ in the *White Crucifixion* all clearly relate to the persecution of the Jews in Nazi Germany, and it is these events, as well as the Crucifixion, that the patriarchs mourn. Their presence here stems from the popular Jewish legend that, after the destruction of the First Temple, God summoned Moses and the Patriarchs to share His grief, for *they* knew how to mourn.[15] They are joined by the matriarch Rachel, whom the prophets described as mourning the exile and destruction of her children, refusing to be comforted (see Jeremiah 31:14).

This meaning of the painting was immediately understood by certain critics when it was first exhibited. Thus Chagall's Russian friend Alexandre Benois wrote of it:

This painting was undoubtedly conceived in suffering. One feels that. . .something woke him [the artist] with a start, that

he was frightened and revolted by it. It is clear that this vision was provoked by the events of the last years, especially by that untranslatable horror that has spread itself over Chagall's co-religionists. . . . [It] corresponds entirely to the villainy of the epoch in which we live.[16]

It is in this connection that one must view Chagall's use of Jesus in this painting as the crucified Jew. He becomes the very symbol of Jewish martyrdom under the Nazis, and it is as such that Chagall later described him:

For me, Christ has always symbolized the true type of the Jewish martyr. That is how I understood him in 1908 when I used this figure for the first time. . . . It was under the influence of the pogroms. Then I painted and drew him in pictures about ghettos, surrounded by Jewish troubles, by Jewish mothers, running terrified with little children in their arms.[17]

This novel usage of the Crucifixion derives from two separate but related artistic traditions that became popular in the nineteenth century. The most well-known of these utilized elements of Christ's Passion, either within or removed from a biblical context, to symbolize the

FIGURE 5. Marc Chagall. *White Crucifixion*, after 1939 (?). Pencil and pen on paper; 46 x 40.7 cm. Artist's estate. Chagall probably made this sketch of the painting in its original state before he painted over some of its details.

FIGURE 6. The *White Crucifixion* was displayed in the Galerie Mai in Paris from January 26 to February 26, 1940, as documented in this photograph from the journal *Cahiers d'art*. This photograph does not provide conclusive evidence that Chagall altered the *White Crucifixion* before the Galerie Mai exhibition, and comments by a reviewer, appearing in the same issue of *Cahiers d'art*, may be interpreted as evidence that the original details in the painting were still visible. Photo: *Cahiers d'art* 15, 1–2 (1940), p. 34.

sufferings of humanity, especially in times of war. Thus in Goya's *Third of May 1808* (Madrid, Museo del Prado) of 1814, the main victim extends his arms as though he were crucified, and his hands bear the stigmata. This symbolism was revived with a vengeance in 1927 by George Grosz, who portrayed the crucified Christ wearing a soldier's boots and a gas mask to symbolize the martyrdom of soldiers in World War I. His message was accented by the brutal inscription: "Shut your mouth and continue to serve."[18] This symbolism was taken up by anti-Fascist artists in the 1930s: in Germany, in 1933–34, Otto Pankok did a series on the Passion in which he suggested that Christ symbolized the victims of the Nazis by giving Christ "Jewish" and "Gypsy" facial features, as opposed to the "Aryan" physiognomy of his persecutors; while in Italy, in a sketch from 1940, Renato Guttauso actually drew Hitler at the foot of the cross.[19]

The second artistic tradition involves the use of Christological symbolism by Jewish artists and is based on ideas current since the mid-eighteenth century in both Jewish and Christian theology, which stressed that Jesus was an orthodox Jew who had come first specifically to his own people.[20] These ideas were given artistic expression in 1873 by two Jewish sculptors, the Russian Mark Antokolsky and the American Moses Jacob Ezekiel. Antokolsky's *Ecce Homo* (fig. 7) depicts Jesus with

Jewish facial features, side curls, a skullcap, and an ancient "Jewish" costume culled from a book on historical dress. Antokolsky's letters to his friends make it clear that the sculpture was inspired not only by theological ideas current at the time, but by the pogroms that shook Russia in 1871, after a period of relative calm. In this work, he tried to remind Christians that Jesus was a Jew, and that the persecution of his brethren was an anti-Christian act, a perversion of Jesus's teachings. His later depictions of Christ are also, for the most part, reactions to anti-Semitic acts and pogroms in Russia.[21] Ezekiel's relief *Israel* (fig. 8) approaches the question from a different angle. Here Christ, crucified on a Y-shaped cross, is surrounded by allegorical figures: Israel, on the right, raises his eyes to heaven in complaint while clenching his

FIGURE 7. Mark Antokolsky (Russian, 1834–1902). *Ecce Homo*, 1873. Marble. Moscow, Tretyakov Gallery. This sculpture and Moses Jacob Ezekiel's *Israel* (fig. 8) are works by Jewish artists that, like Chagall's *White Crucifixion*, use Christian imagery. Both Antokolsky and Ezekiel employed the figure of Christ to symbolize the persecution of Jews; for these artists, as well as for Chagall, acts of anti-Semitism were resolutely anti-Christian in nature.

FIGURE 8. Moses Jacob Ezekiel (American, 1844–1917). *Israel*, 1873. Bronze relief; 144.8 x 113.7 cm. Los Angeles, Hebrew Union College Skirball Museum.

fist in desperate resistance; on the left, Jerusalem wears a crown depicting a walled city as she sits bent over in mourning; and, behind Christ, the last Jewish king holds a broken scepter. It is from his spilled blood, according to the artist, that the tree that becomes Christ's cross has grown.[22] However, since Ezekiel carved the name "Israel" on the base directly under the cross, it seems to refer to Christ himself rather than to any of the other figures, so that the artist seems to suggest not only that Christ is Jewish, but that Israel is Christ crucified. These works inaugurated a long series of Christological paintings by Jewish artists, most of which were reactions to anti-Semitic outbursts and pogroms.[23]

These traditions, especially the Jewish ones, were well known to Chagall. He suggested that a Jewish

artist's goal in Russia was to be a future Antokolsky, and he was himself a protégé of Antokolsky's assistant and close friend, Ilya Ginzberg, who regaled Chagall with tales concerning the master. Chagall was undoubtedly acquainted with Antokolsky's works, which were on exhibit in St. Petersburg while Chagall was studying there, and he could easily have read that artist's published letters, which explained the ideas behind his *Ecce*

FIGURE 9. Marc Chagall. *Golgotha*, 1912. Oil on canvas; 174 x 191 cm. New York, The Museum of Modern Art, Lillie P. Bliss bequest. In this painting and its preliminary sketch (fig. 10), Chagall portrayed the innocent Christ Child as crucified to suggest the victimization of innocent Jews in Russia during the early twentieth century.

FIGURE 10. Marc Chagall. *Sketch for "Golgotha,"* c. 1908/12. Pen on paper. Present whereabouts unknown.

Homo.[24] He was equally acquainted with Ezekiel's *Israel*, which had been reproduced in the December 1903 issue of *Ost und West*, a magazine on Jewish art and culture that had a pronounced effect on Chagall as a young man.[25]

Their approach may have influenced his early *Golgotha* of 1912 (fig. 9), also entitled *Dedicated to Christ*, and its undated preliminary sketch (fig. 10), which Chagall later suggested was drawn in Russia before he moved to Paris.[26] In this unusual depiction of the scene, the crucified victim is the innocent Christ Child rather than the mature Jesus. The painting was executed when it was feared in the West that pogroms were about to break out again in Russia because of the Beilis affair. Mendel Beilis, a Jew, had been arrested in July 1911, accused of murdering a Christian child in order to use his blood for ritual purposes, in accordance with medieval blood libels. The two years he spent in jail before his trial in the fall of 1913 called forth displays of anti-Semitism in Russia, and a strong outcry in the West against these abuses and against the very idea of the blood libel. This revival of the blood libel that had also been a leitmotif of the pogroms of 1904–06, of which Chagall had been only too aware, helps to explain the depiction of the crucified *child*.[27] The

sketch (fig. 10), which may have been related to the original pogroms or to the Beilis trial, depicts a child bleeding copiously from his wounds, while at his feet stand two saints, one of them a Russian bishop.[28] Yet, by substituting his own first name in Hebrew above what appears to be the Russian INRI inscription at the top of the cross, Chagall made it clear that the child is not Christian but Jewish. The sketch thus reverses the blood libel: it is the Jewish child, Chagall-Jesus, who is killed for ritual reasons by the Christians; it is the Jewish child from whom the ladder of the Descent from the Cross is removed in the painting, so that he must remain crucified forever.

This interpretation is borne out by a 1912 sketch for the cross and the landscape in *Golgotha*, which was found on the back of a contemporary sketch for *Adam and Eve* (New York, Hans S. Edersheim Collection). At the bottom of it, Chagall wrote in Russian: "Landscape of blood and of death."[29] In the painting (fig. 9), the blood has drained out of the blue child into the brilliant red ground, which is literally drenched with blood. At the foot of the cross, the Russian saints have been replaced by the child's Jewish parents. His bearded father wears a fringed stole, which recalls the traditional prayer shawl and is visible below his hands, while the mother

FIGURE 11. Marc Chagall. *Crucifixion Seen through a Window*, 1930. Pen, ink, and color on vellum paper; 25.4 x 20.3 cm. Present whereabouts unknown. As in earlier works (see figs. 9–10), Chagall emphasized here the identification of Christ as Jewish. In this instance, the crucified Christ wears a Jewish prayer shawl in place of the more traditional loincloth.

exposes her breast to succor her suffering child.[30] Yet the blue child is no longer suffering. Drained of his life's blood, he slowly becomes detached from his brown cross, absorbed into a green and golden halo as though he were soaring heavenward in an apotheosis. He moves away from his parents, as does the equally blue-garbed figure in the boat with a blue sail. As in many of his paintings from this period, Chagall concealed a personal and bitter message under a seemingly purely spiritual and poetic theme, so that only those who shared the same type of associations and reactions would understand his meaning.[31]

This painting also has another level of meaning stemming from Chagall's identification with the crucified child in the sketch.[32] His placement of his name above the cross suggests his awareness of such art-historical precedents as the crucifixions of James Ensor, who also replaced the INRI sign with his own name.[33] Whereas Ensor saw himself as martyred by the art establishment

that rejected him, Chagall's identification with the martyred child can be partially explained by his contact with anti-Semitism and pogroms in his own childhood. Moreover, the artist left Russia in August 1910, shortly after major Russian cities had begun deporting Jewish "illegal residents" such as Chagall, who had been imprisoned in St. Petersburg for traveling without a pass.[34] Thus, in *Golgotha*, the blue figure in the sailboat hoping to find refuge from Russia and its pogroms is thematically linked to the blue sufferer on the cross.

Both of these meanings—the political and the personal—would recur when Chagall returned to the Crucifixion theme in the 1930s. The connection between *Golgotha* and these later works, especially on the political level, is made clear by Chagall himself: "The Crucifixions I painted from 1908–12 up to these last times, had for me a meaning of human decadence [*déchéance*] rather than a dogmatic meaning."[35] The fact that there was a political meaning involved in *Golgotha* is also suggested by the fact that Chagall only returned to the theme when he became frightened once more by anti-Semitic outbreaks, this time in Germany.

The earliest of these later works appears to be a 1930 drawing of a bearded Jesus whose loincloth is a striped prayer shawl with corner fringes (fig. 11). He is crucified in the landscape of Peyra-Cava in southern France, which can be seen through a window.[36] To understand the sudden appearance of this image with its clear identification of Christ as a Jew, one must realize that Chagall had spent part of the spring of 1930 in Berlin, where he was undoubtedly struck by the threatening atmosphere there. He would later learn of the events of October 15, 1930, the day the Reichstag opened, when the windows of Jewish stores were broken. This occurred when Chagall was in Peyra-Cava, and it accounts both for his return to the Crucifixion theme after almost twenty years and for his use of the tradition that stressed Jesus's Judaism. The windows broken in the pogrom also gave a new meaning to the window motif Chagall had used in his Peyra-Cava

works, and led him to emphasize the window as a literal and figurative frame for the Crucifixion.[37] In this case, the setting of the cross outside the area inhabited by Chagall can also be interpreted as expressing both his feeling of safety from what was happening beyond the borders of France, and the threat it posed to himself as a Jew, as it was clearly perceptible from his "window."

Chagall's approach to this theme was strengthened in 1931, when he visited Palestine in preparation for his work on the Old Testament, traveling with Edmund Fleg, the French writer who is said to have rehabilitated Jesus for the Jews.[38] Fleg, a Jewish theologian, had gone to Palestine to write a life of Christ and, in 1933, published *Jésus raconté par le juif errant*. Like Chagall, Fleg fused the Crucifixion with the suffering of the Jews over the centuries, writing that the Jewish thieves who were cru-

FIGURE 12. Marc Chagall. *Sketch after "The Falling Angel,"* 1934. Gouache on paper; 37 x 48.5 cm. Private collection.

cified along with Jesus were more worthy of pity than he was:

But he, the "Son of God," how long did he have to endure on the cross? Six hours. . . . And the sons of Israel, on his right, on his left, it is almost twenty centuries that they have been nailed to their crosses in his name — nor will they be taken down from them tomorrow.[39]

Whereas Fleg saw the thieves as paradigmatic of Jewish martyrdom, Chagall preferred the image of Christ himself in this role, as we have seen in his 1930 sketch (fig. 11). He continued to use Christ's Passion and Crucifixion in this context in sketches that derive from his 1933 version of *The Falling Angel* (Basel, Kunstmuseum).[40] In the original painting, a red angel hurtles downward toward a sleeping village, a clock on his wing suggesting that time is running out. His motion causes a Jew clutching a Torah scroll and an airborne figure with a cane to flee the scene. In the 1934 sketch (fig. 12), the Jew is joined by a whole company of refugees who flee a

pogrom, symbolized by a burning village and crucifixions in the background.[41] Yet, for the time being, Chagall employed this Christological imagery only in his sketches, and it would take the constantly worsening state of affairs in Germany to make him decide to proclaim these images in a more public way in the *White Crucifixion* of 1938.

This decision was prompted by several considerations. First of all, Chagall may have heard of the scandal revolving around Otto Pankok's *Passion* series in Germany in 1936, where its exhibition and publication had been banned because the artist was accused of incorrectly portraying Christ as a Jew rather than as an Aryan![42] More important, however, was the strong encouragement Chagall received in France itself through the publication in 1937 of Joseph Bonsirven's *Les Juifs et Jésus*, which reviewed modern attitudes toward Christ, a book he probably knew through his close friendship with Jacques and Raïssa Maritain, both of whom were deeply involved in Catholic circles. Bonsirven, a Jesuit, quoted portions

FIGURE 13. Marc Chagall. *Crucifixion*, c. 1940. Oil on canvas; 43.8 x 36.5 cm. New York, private collection. Here Chagall portrayed Christ wearing a skullcap, and replaced the traditional INRI sign at the top of the cross with the Ten Commandments, thereby making the identification of Christ as a Jew even stronger than in the earlier *White Crucifixion* (fig. 1). While the *White Crucifixion* held out hope for some form of escape for the Jews, this later, darker *Crucifixion* does not.

FIGURE 14. Marc Chagall. *The Way to Calvary*, 1941. Wash on paper; 33 x 39.5 cm. Present whereabouts unknown.

of Max Hunterberg's evocatively titled 1927 book *The Crucified Jew*. Bonsirvan also made several statements of his own that probably influenced Chagall: he repeated the argument that Jesus was a Jew and stated that if he came again, he would come to the Jews and pray in their synagogues. Moreover, he made the identification between Jesus and the Jews even stronger by quoting the English novelist and playwright Israel Zangwill: Jews are not only "the People of Christ, but the Christ of the peoples." Bonsirven added: "Like Jesus, the Jews have not ceased to mount Golgotha; like him, they are always nailed to the cross."[43] Bonsirven's words aptly describe Chagall's Crucifixions, and may well have influenced him to treat the subject of the persecution of Jews more openly in his painting.

Chagall's choice of subject also took his intended audience into account. He did not have to explain to Jews what was happening—they already knew. Instead, he wanted to explain the deeper meaning of events in Germany to Christians, and to do so he decided to address them in their own symbolic language, through the use of the Crucifixion. Moreover, his stress on Christ's Judaism is much more visually striking than it had been in the art of Pankok and other anti-Fascist artists. Instead of translating the INRI inscription into the language of the country in which he worked, as Pankok had done, Chagall wrote it in Aramaic so that the letters themselves stress Christ's connection with Judaism, although only those who can read the Hebrew letters can decipher the mes-

sage. The meaning would be conveyed to most Christians through the letters themselves, the inclusion of a prayer shawl as a loincloth, the menorah placed at Christ's feet, the mourning patriarchs above him, and the pogrom scenes around him in the background.

As the situation worsened, Chagall made his meaning increasingly clear, constantly drawing inspiration from events. In a small oil painting of 1940, he painted a variation on the *White Crucifixion* in which he stressed Jesus's Jewishness by setting a skullcap rather than a shawl on his head and by replacing the INRI sign with the Ten Commandments (fig. 13).[44] Jesus is thus completely reassimilated into Judaism, and his crucifixion on a cross bearing the Tablets of the Law suggests that it is *because* he is a Jew that he is being killed. The painting also emphasizes new disasters: the Russians no longer come to the rescue, since they had made peace with Nazi Germany and invaded Poland together in 1939; furthermore, in this variation on the *White Crucifixion*, no ray of light penetrates the darkness of war-torn Europe to illuminate Jesus, and even the candle at the foot of the cross has toppled over. The Torah lies abandoned beside it, no longer rescued by the fleeing Jew, while the synagogue continues to burn at the right. Of the main characters in the foreground of the *White Crucifixion*, only the mother and child at the lower right escape. The refugees on the left fall out of the boat, which has now lost even its one oar, and drown.

In all of these works, the political element rather

FIGURE 15. Marc Chagall, *The Descent from the Cross*, 1941. Gouache on paper; 48.6 x 33 cm. Switzerland, private collection. As in the sketch for *Golgotha* (fig. 10), Chagall substituted his name for the INRI inscription at the top of the cross, identifying himself with the persecuted Christ. In this instance, Chagall was alluding to his recent salvation — that is, his escape from the Nazis and his arrival in New York.

than Chagall's personal identification with Christ is dominant, and this political level of meaning continued to dominate his works throughout the war in such paintings as *The Yellow Crucifixion* and *Obsession* of 1943, and *The Crucified* of 1944.[45] Like these paintings, Chagall's war-time poetry has a political dimension:

A Jew passes with the face of Christ
He cries: Calamity is upon us
Let us run and hide in the ditches.[46]

His 1944 comments to James Johnson Sweeney should also be understood in this light: "For me Christ

was a great poet, *the teaching of whose poetry has been forgotten by the modern world*."[47] This is not just a laudatory remark about Jesus, but a condemnation of the Christian world, which had *forgotten* his teachings, and it echoes the ideas stated both by Jewish theologians and by artists such as Antokolsky.

When Chagall himself was caught up in the Nazi terror and had to flee Paris for New York, however, his more personal identification with Christ came back into play. Thus his fears of deportation are expressed in *The Way to Calvary* sketches of 1941 (see fig. 14), where Christ in his prayer shawl-loincloth is helped on his way by his fellow Jews, several of whom have already been crucified in the burning village in the background. Forcing them to continue, a soldier raises his whip in the gesture of a Nazi beating Jews during a deportation.[48] As Chagall fled that same year, he drew a group of Jewish refugees, some of whom seem to be carrying the crucified Jesus along with them on their flight.[49] In *The Yellow Christ* (c. 1941; private collection), Christ in his prayer shawl-loincloth smiles consolingly at the refugees at his feet who leave the burning village on the right and head for the immigrant ship on the left, stopping for a moment beneath the cross.[50] Finally, on reaching New York, he painted *The Descent from the Cross* (fig. 15), in which Jesus is lowered from a cross whose INRI sign has once more been replaced by the artist's name, "Marc Ch."[51] Held by a bird-headed woman, against a background of the still-smoking Jewish village, Jesus-Chagall is removed from the cross of his suffering. Although he seems to be dead, Chagall obviously hopes to be revived, as an angel with bright blue wings brings him his palette and brushes, calling him back to work.

From this point on, the Crucifixion assumed the double meaning it originally had in the 1912 *Golgotha*: Jesus symbolizes both the artist himself and the fate of the Jewish people. This personal symbolism, which can clearly be seen in works such as *The Painter Crucified*, was also expressed in Chagall's poetry of this period. In one poem, he wrote:

Every day I carry a cross
They push me and drag me by the hand
Already the dark of night surrounds me
You have deserted me, my God? Why?

In another poem, he stated:

I run upstairs
To my dry brushes
And am crucified like Christ
Fixed with nails to the easel.[52]

Whereas this personal meaning became very important in Chagall's postwar paintings, before and during the war Jesus remained predominantly a symbol of Jewish martyrdom, as he had indeed been in the *White Crucifixion*. Considering this painting in its original context makes clear that Chagall was not trying here to depict the Christian Messiah who overcomes all suffering through his sacrifice, but the Jewish martyr who holds out no hope of salvation. Furthermore, this painting shows Chagall to have been as firmly rooted in Jewish traditions of art and iconography as in Christian ones, and to have been aware of, and capable of reacting to, actual political events that moved him.

This painting is, moreover, the first of his biblical works to invoke the principles underlying his postwar Bible series. Previously, he had depicted single biblical scenes both in his paintings and in his etchings for Ambroise Vollard, and he had, with few exceptions, kept within the historical and chronological framework of each scene. In the *White Crucifixion*, Chagall expanded the meaning of the event, not only changing the original biblical image, but placing it in a more clearly modern historical context than had been the case in *Golgotha*. The play in time and space between major and minor scenes became the basis both for his later series of biblical paintings, which he called his *Message biblique*, and for his use of Old and New Testament imagery in his stained-glass windows for churches and his tapestries and mosaics for Jerusalem's Knesset.[53] In these later works, he used a more allegorical manner of connecting the various levels of his message. But in the *White Crucifixion* he preached it loudly and clearly, stating that what was happening in Germany was a recrucifixion of the Jewish Jesus, an act that only a world forgetful of Christ's teachings could tolerate. He wanted this message to be understood by the Christian world, and to have a positive effect on that world's behavior. For this reason, Chagall chose in the *White Crucifixion* not to follow his usual penchant for using his art as a vehicle for personal expression with ambiguous messages that could often be fully understood only by people whose background was similar to his own. On the contrary, he chose clear imagery, hoping that his painting would be a means of political communication with an unresponsive world.

GREGORIUS XIII PONT. OPT. MAX.

A Connoisseur's Montage: The *Four Evangelists* Attributed to Giulio Clovio

SANDRA HINDMAN
Northwestern University
MICHAEL HEINLEN
Lake Forest College

In 1982, The Art Institute of Chicago acquired an important but little-known montage (fig. 1), which was assembled in the nineteenth century out of a set of fragments excised from a lavishly decorated Italian Renaissance manuscript. These fragments are significant, as we will argue, because they can be linked to a group of other similarly excised fragments that originally constituted a substantial portion of the illuminations from an impressive service book, now lost, made for Pope Gregory XIII (reigned 1572–85). The rediscovery of the Art Institute montage enables us to understand better the original appearance of this distinctive manuscript. The montage is also important as an example of highly accomplished sixteenth-century Italian book painting and as a reflection of an emerging taste for manuscript illumination among art collectors in the early nineteenth century. When it first appeared on the market in 1825, it helped to create a demand for Medieval and Renaissance miniatures and, in particular, for the work of Giulio Clovio (1498–1578), to whom it was ascribed. As will be discussed, the style of the painting is, in fact, quite close to the late work of that celebrated miniaturist, whom the Renaissance biographer Giorgio Vasari extolled as a "small and new Michelangelo."[1] Indeed, the Art Institute montage must play an important role in any evaluation of an obscure phase of Clovio's career.

The six cuttings brought together in this montage are all examples of decorative elements that appear frequently in richly illuminated sixteenth-century Italian manuscripts. They include four separate miniatures of the Evangelists, a full-page *trompe l'oeil* border, and an architectural cartouche, which now encloses a nineteenth-century inscription. Originally, these embellished the text on the pages of a sumptuous manuscript, but they have all been carefully cut out and reassembled to form a unified composition resembling an independent painting rather than a page from a book (see fig. 2 for an example of an uncut page from an illuminated manuscript). Arranged clockwise in the center of the montage are the miniatures of the Four Evangelists, accompanied by their symbols: Matthew, gently comforted by an angel, who points to his book; Luke, his hand resting on his head and leaning pensively for support on an ox; John, pointing to his text and looking backward toward Mark, with an eagle nestled beside him; and Mark, quietly

FIGURE 2. Giulio Clovio. *The Head of Lazarus,* c. 1532–37. Tempera on parchment. London, British Library, Stuart de Rothesay Book of Hours (Add. MS. 20927, f. 120). Photo: Maria Cionini-Visani and Grgo Gamulin, *Giorgio Clovio: Miniaturist of the Renaissance* (New York, 1980), p. 32. Unlike the Art Institute's *Four Evangelists* (fig. 1), which was assembled with unrelated parts of an illuminated manuscript, *The Head of Lazarus* is an uncut page created entirely by Clovio. This page suggests what the parts of the Art Institute montage may have looked like within uncut pages featuring scriptural text.

gazing upward, while a lion rests at his feet. Each of the Evangelists is seated in the immediate foreground of an impressionistic open landscape. In three of the four miniatures, the figures are framed on the left by a feathery tree, the profile of which subtly conforms with the contours of the body of the Evangelist. On the right, the Evangelists are framed by rectangular or columnar piers. The imposing, pyramidal forms of the figures, coupled with the soft pastel colors, delicate modeling, and illusionistic backgrounds, create the dual effect of monumentality and preciousness.

A full-page rectangular border surrounds the miniatures. This border is composed primarily of flowers, insects, and birds illusionistically painted against a gold ground. At the top and sides, three oval medallions, depicting personifications of the Seven Virtues, are painted in pastel colors that resemble those used in the miniatures. These personifications of the Seven Virtues—the Three Theological Virtues and the Four Cardinal Virtues—are arranged as follows: left, Faith, holding up a chalice and a host in one hand

and a book in the other, with Hope, hands raised in prayer; right, Fortitude, holding a broken column over her head and trampling broken columns at her feet, with Prudence, a book held in one hand and a serpent entwined around the other; and top, Charity, supporting three children, Justice, with scales and a sword in opposite hands, and Temperance, pouring water into a jug of wine. The style of the border is generally similar to that of the Evangelist miniatures, but the comparatively harsh treatment of the figures in the medallions indicates that it is the work of a second artist.

In the space above the miniatures of the Four Evangelists appears an architectural cartouche, composed of painted stucco-like ornamentation. The cartouche, the border, and the four miniatures are glued to a gold ground, which was painted in the nineteenth century and includes the inscription: GREGORIUS XIII PONT. OPT. MAX ("Pope Gregory XIII"). Although the inscription apparently dates from the period when the montage was put together, it records an original provenance that is confirmed at the bottom of the border by the arms of Pope Gregory XIII, a dragon in an escutcheon, upheld by two putti and surmounted by the papal tiara and keys.

The Art Institute montage belongs with a significant group of similarly excised miniatures and borders, many of which were sold in London in 1825 in one of the first major sales of miniature paintings.[2] At the end of the eighteenth century, thousands of manuscripts were taken from Italian churches that had been nationalized under Napoleon, and many miniatures were imported north to France and England. The "highly valuable and extremely curious" miniatures announced in the 1825 catalogue had themselves been cut from manuscripts stolen from the Sistine Chapel during the Napoleonic invasion of Rome in 1798 and had been brought to England by the Abate Luigi Celotti (c. 1768–c. 1846). Celotti had been secretary and librarian to Count Giovanni Barbarigo in Venice in 1801, and by the 1820s he had become a dealer of miniatures and paintings in France and England.[3] Marketed as examples of the "Art of Painting," the Celotti miniatures were attributed to well-known Italian Renaissance painters, including Andrea Mantegna, Giovanni Bellini, Girolamo dai Libri, and Giulio Clovio, who worked for some of the most famous patrons of the period, including Cardinal Antonio Pallavicini and Popes Leo X, Clement VII, Pius IV, and Gregory XIII. The Art Institute montage was one of four lots reportedly from a manuscript painted by Giulio Clovio for Pope Gregory XIII.

These four lots, 86 to 89, make up the core of a group of ten sets of manuscript fragments described by the scholar T. Julian Brown in 1960, which were probably illuminated for Pope Gregory XIII.[4] Among these ten sets of fragments, Brown was unable to trace the whereabouts of five, including the present montage. He identified the artist of all the fragments as a follower of Clovio, although he worked from incomplete evidence, because the five he was unable to locate each include miniatures. A few other scholars have suggested attributions for individual miniatures from this group, but none has considered the entire group as a whole.[5] Brown, among others, assumed that the fragments came from one or more papal service books, probably an Evangelistary, but no one has systematically evaluated the evidence in an attempt to determine definitively the identity of the book or books and the coherence of the group of fragments.

In the following discussion, we will refine Brown's arguments based on new evidence, of which the discovery of the Art Institute montage is a crucial component. First, we will trace all the remaining fragments (see Appendix, nos. 1–8, 10), except one (see Appendix, no. 9). Second, we will discuss the coherence of this group of fragments in the light of their possible common origin and the present evidence that suggests they all come from a sumptuous papal service book, which was most likely an Evangelistary for Pope Gregory XIII once housed in the Sistine Chapel. Third, we will explain why these fragments have come down to us in their present condition as "independent" works of art and who was interested in collecting them. Fourth, we will reconsider the issue of attribution. The Art Institute montage emerges as historically significant because of its appearance in a celebrated nineteenth-century sale that helped set the fashion for a century of collectors who regarded miniatures as "works of Fine Art." Indeed, as the work of a skilled painter whose style is very close to that of Clovio, if not by Clovio himself, the miniatures in the Art Institute montage still sustain the ambitious claims made for Italian Renaissance miniature painting in the Celotti sale.

As noted, the core of this group comprises four sets of fragments from the Celotti sale. The Celotti catalogue grouped the miniature paintings under headings of the popes from whose service books they were excised. According to the catalogue, lots 86 to 89 "appear to have belonged to a Volume decorated for Pope Gregory XIII." Lot 86 is the leaf in The Art Institute of Chicago (see Appendix, no. 1). Lot 87 is a similar montage (fig. 3), depicting the Four Evangelists surrounded by a floral border, now in the Pierpont Morgan Library, New York (see Appendix, no. 2). Lot 88 is composed of five border fragments (fig. 4) now in a manuscript in the British Library, London (see Appendix, no. 3). Lot 89 is a miniature of the Crucifixion that is in the Brooklyn Museum (fig. 5; see Appendix, no. 4a), now separated from the border that once accompanied it, which is presently located in the British Library (fig. 6; see Appendix, no. 4b).

A review of lots 87–89 may be instructive here. Lot 87, the montage in the Pierpont Morgan Library, is a virtual twin to the Art Institute montage (see figs. 1 and 3). Like the Art Institute montage, it is made up of six parchment cuttings, consisting of four separate miniatures of the Evangelists, a floral border with three oval medallions and the papal arms of Gregory XIII, and an architectural cartouche with a nineteenth-century inscription. Although the Four Evangelists are arranged in a different order (Mark and Luke are reversed), they are unquestionably by the same painter who executed the Art Institute *Evangelists*. They are posed remarkably similarly in open landscapes with identical architectural frames. They display the same reflective moods as they interact with their symbols — for example, Matthew, who is comforted by a diaphanous angel, or Luke, who leans for support on an ox.

The floral border surrounding the Evangelists on the Morgan montage is of a similar type to that in the Art Institute montage, but, as Brown first argued, it does appear to be by the same artist who painted the miniatures. In addition to the flowers, insects, and birds (which are painted without the same illusionism as in the Art Institute montage), the border contains gold cameo medallions, left and right, of the Archangel Gabriel and the Virgin Mary of the Annunciation. At the top is a half-length figure of God the Father as the "Ancient of Days" with his long white hair and flowing beard, a figure that appears frequently in scenes of the Annunciation. The refined treatment of the faces and figures in these medallions, in particular the handling of God the Father, link them stylistically to the Evangelists in the miniatures. The papal arms are upheld by two putti in the lower margin. An architectural cartouche above the miniatures of the Four Evangelists surrounds a nineteenth-century inscription, apparently by the same hand as the

FIGURE 3. Giulio Clovio, follower (?). *Four Evangelists*, c. 1572. Tempera and gold on parchment; 41.3 x 27.7 cm. New York, The Pierpont Morgan Library. © The Pierpont Morgan Library 1991. This montage is remarkably similar to that of the Art Institute (fig. 1), particularly in the style of the four central miniatures (the Evangelists are, clockwise from upper left, Matthew, Mark, John, and Luke). In contrast to the Art Institute montage, the Morgan's features a border that appears to have been executed by the same artist who painted its Evangelists.

GREGORIUS XIII
PONTIFEX OPTIMUS MAXIMUS
BONCOMPAGNUS BONONIENSIS
ELECTUS ANNO DOMINI MDLXXIII.

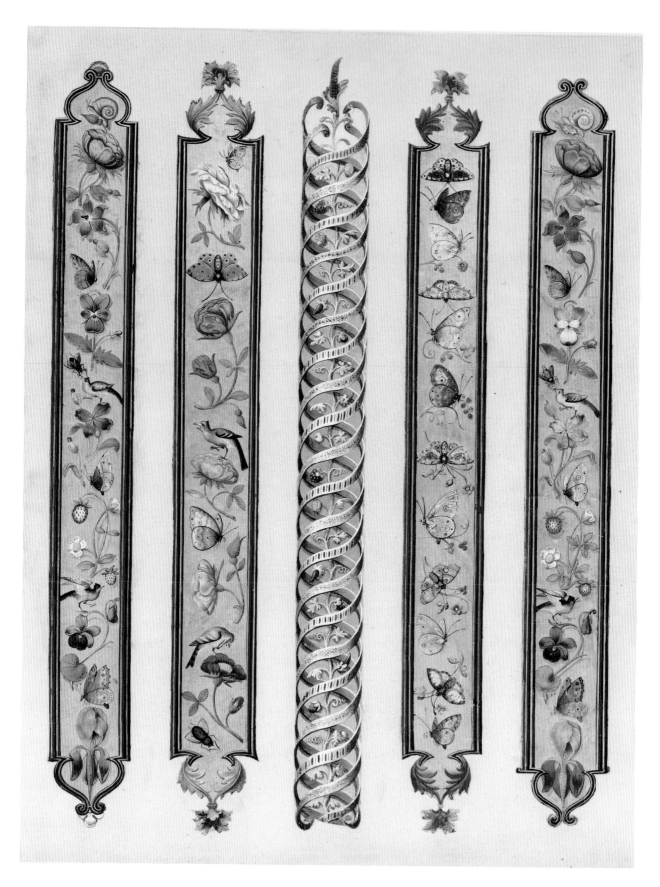

Chicago inscription: GREGORIUS XIII PONTIFEX OPTIMUS MAXIMUS BONCOM-PAGNUS BONONIENSIS ELECTUS ANNO DOMINI MDLXXIII [*sic*] ("Pope Gregory XIII, Buoncompagni of Bologna, elected in the year 1573").

Lot 88 from the Celotti sale, "containing five pieces of border, richly decorated with flowers, birds, and butterflies," is undoubtedly among a group of leaves and cuttings from the collection of John Malcolm of Poltalloch that was given to the British Library (fig. 4).[6] According to Brown, with whom we concur, it is by the same artist who executed the Art Institute *Evangelists* and both the border and the *Evangelists* of the Morgan montage.

Whereas Brown was able to trace only the border of lot 89, we have identified the miniature as well (fig. 5). The border (fig. 6), described in the Celotti catalogue as being "decorated at the corners by four female Masks; and containing also, four compartments, in which are the whole-length Figures of the Evangelists, with their Symbolic accompaniments," has been identified, along with Celotti lot 88, in the collection of John Malcolm of Poltalloch. The miniature of the *Crucifixion*, cursorily described in the catalogue as a "composition of eight figures," is now in the Brooklyn Museum. It includes the Roman soldier Longinus standing at the far right, Mary Magdalen kneeling at the foot of the cross, and the swooning Virgin Mary supported by John the Evangelist in the left foreground. Three of the other Galilean women present at the Crucifixion, including Mary, mother of James and Joseph, and Salome, wife of Zebedee, are also shown to the left and right of the cross. A sweeping mountainous landscape recedes to reveal the walled city of Jerusalem in the distance behind the cross. At the foot of the cross appears the skull of Adam, which indicates that the Crucifixion took place at the site of Adam's grave and was meant to signify the power of Christ's death to redeem the original sin of Adam. The Brooklyn Museum miniature, the only full-page miniature in the set, is by a distinct artist who does not appear to have been responsible for anything else in the group. The border, however, is by the painter responsible for the Art Institute *Evangelists*.

Although not included in Celotti's sale, six other cuttings or groups of cuttings of both borders and miniatures probably had the same origin as lots 86–89. Brown had seen three of the six groups, the identities of which we therefore will only briefly summarize. In the album of Samuel Rogers, there are thirteen borders (see Appendix, no. 10). Two of these are painted by the artist of the Chicago *Evangelists* (fig. 7a,b; see Appendix, no. 10a). Along with these, eleven other borders (see fig. 8a–d) share nearly the same dimensions as all the borders so far discussed, and some bear the arms or name of Pope Gregory XIII (see Appendix, no. 10b). Among the group of fragments given to the British Library by John Malcolm of Poltalloch is another montage composed of a border of arabesques and seated figures of a pope, a cardinal, and two bishops that surrounds two miniatures of the *Last Supper* and *Angels Adoring the Host* (fig. 9; see Appendix, no. 5). The dimensions of this border are similar to those in the rest of the group, and both the border and the miniatures are by the same hand as the Art Institute *Evangelists*. There is also another miniature in the British Library of *Saint Matthew*, which is by the same artist who painted the Art Institute *Evangelists* and is of comparable dimensions (fig. 10; see Appendix, no. 7).

Untraced by Brown are three miniatures of the Evangelists: Saint Luke, Saint John, and another rendering of Saint Matthew. We have located two of these previously missing miniatures in American collections: *Saint Luke* in the Free Library in Philadelphia (fig. 11; see Appendix, no. 6) and *Saint John* in a private collection in Texas (fig. 12; see Appendix, no. 8). As in the

FIGURE 4. Giulio Clovio, follower (?). *Ornamental border fragments*, c. 1572. Tempera on parchment; 38.7 x 28.9 cm. London, British Library (Add. MS. 35254.N). By permission of the British Library.

Chicago and Morgan montages, each Evangelist is displayed in an open landscape and seated next to his appropriate symbol. Near-identical architectural details appear on the right in each miniature. Stylistic and compositional similarities extend even to the exact contours and drapery of Saint John, who, as the art historian Harry Bober noticed, repeats the pattern of the Morgan *Saint Matthew*.[7]

There is strong evidence to suggest that this entire group of fragments, including the components of the Art Institute montage, was taken from a lavishly illustrated papal service book recorded in inventories of the Sistine Chapel as an Evangelistary of Pope Gregory XIII. If we assume that Celotti, who probably brought the cuttings from Italy to England, was aware of their actual origin, then the evidence in the Celotti catalogue needs to be taken seriously. The catalogue groups these four lots together as having belonged to

FIGURE 5. Giulio Clovio, follower (?). *Crucifixion*, c. 1472. Tempera on parchment; 23.7 x 14.7 cm. New York, Brooklyn Museum, Gift of A. Augustus Healy (11.499). By permission of the Brooklyn Museum. This is the only full-page miniature in the set of works considered here, and it was created by an artist who apparently was not responsible for anything else in the group.

FIGURE 6. Giulio Clovio, follower (?). *Ornamental border*, c. 1572. Tempera on parchment; 35.6 x 26.4 cm. London, British Library (Add. MS. 35254.P). By permission of the British Library. This border was once joined to the *Crucifixion* (fig. 5) after both pieces were cut from the stolen Evangelistary of Pope Gregory XIII. The same artist who painted this border also painted the Evangelists of the Art Institute montage (fig. 1). There is a notable similarity in the refined handling of figures in both works.

a single book made for Pope Gregory XIII.[8] Apart from this evidence, there is corroborating physical evidence from the fragments themselves. Many of these, as we have seen, display the arms and name of the pope. In addition, they exhibit an extraordinary degree of uniformity of style, composition, and dimensions. The sum of the evidence thus points to their common origin in a single book. The illumination of luxury manuscripts was often a collaborative enterprise involving the cooperation of several artists. The lavishly illustrated Towneley Lectionary, for example, contains numerous miniatures and elaborate border decorations by several different artists, including Clovio, who painted four of the full-page miniatures (see fig. 14).[9] Therefore, it is not problematic that the Brooklyn *Crucifixion* and a number of the borders, including that of the Art Institute montage, were painted by different artists than the majority of the remaining miniatures and borders in the group.

Two unpublished inventories of the Sistine Chapel compiled in the eighteenth century, as Mirella Levi d'Ancona pointed out, mention an *Evangelistario di Papa Gregorio 13°* containing forty-nine leaves, of which twenty were "bonissime miniate" ("very well illuminated").[10] An Evangelistary is a

FIGURE 7 a,b. Giulio Clovio, follower (?).
Ornamental border fragments, c. 1572. Tempera
on parchment; a: 34 x 4; b: 35 x 3.8 cm.
London, British Library (Add. MS. 21412, f. 50,
nos. 109–10). By permission of the British
Library. These border fragments and the
following ones (fig. 8) were cut from the stolen
Evangelistary, but were never assembled to
form new works, and therefore remain cuttings.

FIGURE 8 a,b,c,d. Giulio Clovio, follower (?).
Ornamental border fragments, c. 1572.
Tempera on parchment; a: 35 x 4; b: 35 x 3.8;
c: 35.3 x 3.8; d: 35 x 3.8 cm. London, British
Library (Add. MS. 21412, ff. 46–49, nos. 100,
102, 104, 106).

FIGURE 9. Giulio Clovio, follower (?). *Last Supper* and *Angels Adoring the Host* with Ornamental Border Fragment, c. 1572. Tempera on parchment; 34.5 x 26 cm. London, British Library (Add. MS. 35254.K). By permission of the British Library.

service book that includes the readings from the Gospels appropriate for the feasts of the liturgical year as recited by the celebrant at the Mass. Like the Evangelistary written for Cardinal Marino Grimani in 1528 and illustrated by Clovio, an illuminated Evangelistary includes multiple miniatures of the Evangelists, introducing different readings from the Gospels, as well as miniatures appropriate to the individual feasts.[11] It is evident, therefore, that the group of fragments discussed in this essay, comprising twelve miniatures of the Evangelists, three miniatures of feasts (Maundy Thursday, Good Friday, and Corpus Christi),[12] and numerous borders and border fragments, were once combined with text leaves in a sumptuous Evangelistary. This is substantiated by the fragmentary text on the verso of the miniature of *Saint Matthew* in the British Library. This text includes a portion of the Gospel reading for All Saints's Day (November 1), a passage from the Sermon on the Mount as recounted in Matthew's Gospel.[13] It seems likely, then, that the total group of fifteen miniatures, along with the borders and border fragments, may well comprise three-quarters of the illustrations from the twenty "very well illuminated" pages of Pope Gregory's Evangelistary.

This Evangelistary is undoubtedly one of the volumes stolen from the Sistine Chapel in 1798 and subsequently dismembered. Along with a group of ninety-seven miniatures mostly from papal books in the Vatican, the Art Institute montage was acquired by Celotti, who set out to market them to dealers and collectors of Old Master paintings. In his capacity as secretary and librarian in Venice from 1801, Celotti had ready entry into Italian collections, and by 1825 he had purchased numerous books and manuscripts from the monastic libraries of Santa Giustina in Padua and San Giorgio Maggiore in Venice, from the Jesuits of Tours, and from private collectors, such as Matteo Luigi Canonici, Giovanni Saibante, Giacomo Nani, Giovanni Salviati, Scipione Maffei, and Don Tomaso da Lucca.[14] He sold 4,000 of these books in three separate sales in 1825 at Sotheby's in London,[15] but he chose Christie's to handle the auction of his miniature paintings, dating from the fifteenth through the seventeenth centuries, apparently because this firm was then better known among picture dealers.[16]

Written in 1825, the catalogue of the Celotti sale of miniatures was evidently aimed at this audience. To write the catalogue, Christie's employed William Young Ottley, an art historian who had studied at the Royal Academy and had spent ten years in Italy, and whose publications on Italian art, particularly on Italian primitives, were already well known and widely respected.[17] In fact, the title page of the catalogue implied that Ottley, "a gentleman well conversant in the History of early Italian Art," legitimized

FIGURE 10. Giulio Clovio, follower (?). *Saint Matthew*, c. 1572. Tempera on parchment; 10.5 x 10.5 cm. London, British Library (Add. MS. 49520). By permission of the British Library.

FIGURE 11. Giulio Clovio, follower (?). *Saint Luke*, c. 1572. Tempera on parchment; 8 x 8 cm. Free Library of Philadelphia, Rare Book Department (MS. 27:7). By permission of the Free Library. Photo: Joan Broderick. There are many stylistic and compositional similarities between the Art Institute's *Four Evangelists*, this miniature of *Saint Luke*, and the following *Saint John the Evangelist* (fig. 12), which lead to the conclusion that they were painted by the same hand.

the project. Leaving no doubt as to his participation, Ottley signed the introduction. In that introduction, called an "Advertisement," Ottley made it clear that these miniature paintings were to be considered alongside "frescoes and other large works of painting remaining to us of the same periods" as superior examples of the "style of Art that prevailed at the times." Ottley's frequent reliance on Vasari as an authority, and his eagerness to relate miniature painters, such as Clovio, to monumental painters, such as Michelangelo, Raphael, and Giulio Romano, provide clear examples of his strategy. He also called attention to the additional importance of miniature paintings, when compared with the monumental arts, by noting their "more perfect state of preservation." Organized in chronological order, with detailed historical notes, attributions to major artists, and elaborate descriptions, the catalogue displayed an unprecedented degree of sophistication that reinforced the perception of miniatures as legitimate examples of the "Art of Painting in Italy."

The success of the Celotti catalogue can be measured by the relatively high prices paid, which were comparable to those paid for Old Master paintings.[18] Sixteenth-century miniatures by well-known painters fetched the highest prices. For example, a large miniature of "unparalleled magnificence" of the *Crucifixion*, which was signed by Apollonius de Bonfratelli, whose "style is decidedly an imitation of that of Michelangiolo," set the record for the sale at £91 (lot 85). The Brooklyn Museum *Crucifixion* attributed to Clovio and belonging to our group realized the second highest price at £38 17s. (lot 89). Comparable prices were paid for other works by Bonfratelli, whose many signed full-page miniatures realized overall the highest prices, and by Clovio, whose miniatures ranged from £16 16s. to £38 17s. The Art Institute of Chicago montage was sold for £16 16s. A miniature by Girolamo dai Libri, whom Vasari identified as the teacher of Clovio, brought a similarly high price, £17 66s. (lot 56), and two miniatures by an artist "of superior talent" whose style was related to Andrea Mantegna's were sold for £38 10s. and £29 8s. (lots 38 and 40). The entire sale made nearly £800.

Prosperous dealers of Old Master paintings turned up at the Celotti sale and bought heavily. One-quarter of the lots, or twenty-four miniatures, were acquired by Antony Molteno (died c. 1846), a collector and dealer of prints and drawings and an associate of the celebrated London firm Colnaghi's, which handled fine paintings.[19] Molteno set all the records at the sale and obtained every high-priced miniature. William Manson (died 1852), who would later join forces with James Christie but at this time was an independent picture dealer, bought ten lots. Among London booksellers, only Robert Triphook successfully purchased a few relatively inexpensive lots. Other buyers included connoisseurs and collectors. For example, Ottley himself, who had amassed a major collection of paintings, forty-nine of which he sold in May 1801 at Christie's, bought fifteen lots in his own name, and he appears to have subsequently owned many of the miniatures purchased by Molteno, who may thus have bought for him.[20] In fact, Ottley owned both the Art Institute and Pierpont Morgan Library montages, which he probably acquired from Molteno, who bought them in the sale. Samuel Rogers, poet-laureate, dilettante, and collector of paintings, engravings, antiquities, and books, also purchased in his own name, buying three miniatures, including one of the sets of borders belonging to our group (lot 88, £9).

Collectors at the Celotti sale viewed sixteenth-century miniatures as small-scale monumental paintings, and they made their purchases against the backdrop of the broader history of taste and collecting during roughly the first half of the nineteenth century. One of the earliest histories of manuscript illumination published in England, Sir Frederic Madden and Henry

FIGURE 12. Giulio Clovio, follower (?).
Saint John the Evangelist, c. 1572.
Tempera on parchment; 8 x 8.2 cm. Texas, private collection.

Shaw's *Illuminated Ornaments Selected from Manuscripts and Early Printed Books from the Sixth to the Sixteenth Centuries* (London, 1830–33), succinctly summarizes this attitude.[21] Madden, author of the text and Assistant Keeper, then Keeper, of Manuscripts at the British Museum, held that the art of illumination gradually advanced in perfection from the eighth to the sixteenth centuries, triumphing in the miniatures of "Julio Clovio." Art of earlier periods showed "false taste," "deterioration," and "excesses of extravagance," whereas miniature painting in the sixteenth century "received a new degree of lustre and dignity" from having been practiced by artists like Leonardo da Vinci and Raphael.

This attitude began to change with the next generation of collectors, who bought from Ottley, Rogers, and others in the middle of the nineteenth century. People such as William Horatio Crawford of Lakelands (died c. 1891), Lord John Rushout of Northwick Park (1770–1859), and John Malcolm of Poltalloch (1805–1893), all of whom owned miniatures from our group (see Appendix, nos. 3, 5, 6, and 7), exhibited what can best be described as a Victorian attitude toward collecting. Collectors, such as the unidentified individual who bought many of Rogers's borders in 1856, began assembling miniatures as collectibles in albums, instead of displaying them on walls as mini-easel paintings.[22] Following the lead of the Victorian collector and critic of art John Ruskin, who passionately refuted each of Madden's points outlined above, collectors now also sought earlier "Gothic" miniatures, which they appreciated as examples of illustrations from manuscript books.[23] By the end of the century, collectors no longer viewed miniature painting as small-scale monumental painting, and as a result the work of Clovio began to fall out of fashion.[24]

Yet another generation of collectors ensured the diffusion and relocation of many of these miniatures, including those from our group, to this country. Following the economic panic of 1893, a new era of financial prosperity in the United States brought wealthy Americans to Europe on buying sprees.[25] In the late 1890s, for example, the financier J. Pierpont Morgan began to travel extensively in Europe, buying at auction and privately, eventually purchasing the New York montage (fig. 3). Around the same time, John Frederick Lewis, a lawyer from Philadelphia, bought nearly two thousand leaves and cuttings, which he eventually bequeathed to the Free Library of Philadelphia. Among these were the miniature of *Saint Luke* from our group and three Bonfratelli miniatures, of which one, the *Deposition from the Cross* (fig. 13), came from the Celotti sale (lot 84). Coella Lindsay Ricketts, a practicing calligrapher and illuminator in Chicago, also bought about seven hundred leaves and cuttings, including a set of borders by Bonfratelli from the Celotti sale (lot 44).[26]

From the initial appearance of the core of our group of fragments on the market in London in 1825 to their accession in American collections in this century, when they have been most closely studied, there has been surprising agreement on their attribution (for summaries, see Appendix). Prior to 1937, all published references to fragments in the group (the Art Institute montage dropped out of the literature after the Ottley sale until very recently) concurred with the attribution to Clovio. Around 1937, apparently following Belle da Costa Greene, Seymour De Ricci first introduced the name of Apollonio de Bonfratelli, to whom he attributed the Morgan montage (see Appendix, no. 2). At the same time, De Ricci maintained the attribution of the Brooklyn *Crucifixion* to Clovio (see Appendix, no. 5). From 1937 until around 1960 and apparently following De Ricci and Greene, the Morgan

FIGURE 13. Apollonio de Bonfratelli (Italian, active 1523–72). *Deposition from the Cross,* 1571. Tempera and gold on parchment; 48.3 x 39.4 cm. Philadelphia, Rosenbach Museum and Library (54.663). By permission of the Rosenbach Museum and Library. In the past, scholars have attributed works by Clovio or his followers to Bonfratelli. A comparison of Bonfratelli's *Deposition* and Clovio's *Adoration of the Shepherds* (fig. 14), however, makes clear the stylistic differences between the two artists. The haggard faces of Bonfratelli's despairing figures are completely unlike the more serene expressions of Clovio's figures.

montage was unanimously assigned to Bonfratelli. Then, without offering supporting arguments, scholars since about 1960, beginning with Brown, have reversed the attribution to Bonfratelli and have classified the Morgan montage as a work by a follower of Clovio. Brown mentioned the formative influence of Matteo da Milano on our artist, whom he concluded "owes much to Clovio." In discussing the Morgan montage, Gregory Clark and William Voelkle, who also knew of the Art Institute montage, suggested that the style of the common artist of the two montages "is clearly indebted to that of Clovio." Since its acquisition of the montage under discussion here, the Art Institute has maintained the attribution to Clovio and has published it as such.[27] But for Brown and other recent scholars, "neither cap fits,"[28] and there the argument inconclusively rests. In what follows, we will reevaluate these attributions and argue that although an attribution to Clovio remains problematic, the style of the miniatures in this group, including the Art Institute montage, is actually remarkably close to that of his known late works, and that the outright rejection of Clovio as the artist responsible for them is equally troublesome.

We believe we can dispense once and for all with the attribution to Apollonio de Bonfratelli of miniatures in this group. He referred to himself as "Apollonius de Bonfratellis de Capranica, Capellae et Sacristiae Apostolicae Miniator" ("Apollonio de Bonfratelli of Capranica, miniaturist of the Apostolic Chapel and Sacristy").[29] As this title implies, he apparently worked for successive popes from about 1523 to 1572. For example, miniatures by him in the Celotti sale were painted for Popes Paul IV, Pius IV, and Pius V, and date from 1558 to 1572. He often signed his works, sometimes with the initials A.P.F. ("Apollonio Bonfratelli fecit"), and the nineteenth-century inscriptions that accompany many of his miniatures and borders are said to be, like the inscriptions recording the patronage of Pope Gregory XIII on the Art Institute montage, "correctly copied from corresponding inscriptions originally existing in the Books themselves."[30]

Bonfratelli is undoubtedly close to Clovio, for they shared with Michelangelo an interest in muscular anatomy, with Pontormo an interest in variegated colors, and with Raphael an interest in tender expressions. His debt to Clovio extends to his incorporation of vignettes modeled from antique gems in the borders and his use of soft impressionistic landscapes in the background of his miniatures. What is distinctive about Bonfratelli's style, however, can be readily perceived on examination of a signed miniature of the *Deposition from the Cross*, which is dated 1571 and comes from the Celotti sale, lot 84 (fig. 13).[31] When compared with a datable Clovio from the same period, the Towneley Lectionary (fig. 14),[32] it is evident that in Bonfratelli's *Deposition from the Cross* the exaggerated anatomy is toned down, the colors are more highly saturated, and the faces are distinctive and unmistakable, painted with wedge-shaped contours, deep-set hollow eyes, and long pointed noses. No miniature in our group of fragments displays these singular features.

Instead, our miniatures have much in common with the style of Giulio Clovio, Vasari's "small and new Michelangelo." Clovio's life and works are relatively well documented.[33] Born in Croatia in 1498, he was in the service of Cardinal Marino Grimani in 1516 in Venice, where he purportedly learned the art of illumination. He traveled to Rome in 1526, Mantua in 1527 (where he saw his friend Giulio Romano), and Padua in 1530 (where he met Girolamo dai Libri), eventually settling in Rome first in 1537 and then permanently in 1560–61, residing in the Palazzo Farnese until his death in 1578.

FIGURE 14. Giulio Clovio. *Adoration of the Shepherds*, 1568/77. Tempera on parchment; 48.3 x 32.7 cm. New York Public Library, Rare Books and Manuscripts Division, Astor, Lenox and Tilden Foundations (De Ricci MS. 91 [The Towneley Lectionary], f. 5v). By permission of the New York Public Library.

There are four documented works by Clovio, of which only two are dated: the Farnese Hours of 1546 (New York, Pierpont Morgan Library, M.69), and the Uffizi *Crucifixion* of 1553.[34] Nevertheless, we can easily sketch out the major outlines of his career, as Mirella Levi d'Ancona has done.[35] Early in his career, he painted the Grimani Evangelistary, written in 1528, and the Stuart de Rothesay Hours (London, British Library, Add. MS 20927), possibly illuminated between 1532 and 1537. Following these works are the Farnese Hours and the signed *Crucifixion*. Clovio's late career is most difficult to define. Levi d'Ancona argued for a late date for the Towneley Lectionary, with two datable miniatures before 1568 and two others between 1568 and 1577.[36] She claimed that because Giorgio Vasari in his 1568 edition of the *Lives* did not refer to two of the miniatures in the Towneley Lectionary, which do appear in Clovio's inventory at his death in 1577, these miniatures are by Clovio but after 1568. Acceptance of Levi d'Ancona's argument means that the miniatures of the *Adoration of the Shepherds* and the *Resurrection* become benchmarks for the style of Clovio late in his career.[37]

Similarities between the *Adoration of the Shepherds* from the Towneley Lectionary and the miniatures in our group of fragments are immediately apparent. All these miniatures exhibit the same pale tonality, exaggerated muscular forms, and soft impressionistic landscapes. The figures are depicted in intense introspective emotional states. There are certain telling details that link even more closely the *Adoration of the Shepherds* and our group of miniatures: for example, the virtually identical faces of the seated figure of Joseph in the *Adoration of the Shepherds* and Saint Mark in the Pierpont Morgan montage (figs. 14 and 3). Joseph's pose is likewise very similar to those of Saint John in the Pierpont Morgan montage and Saint Luke in the Art Institute montage (figs. 14, 3, and 1). Furthermore, the face of the kneeling shepherd depicted in profile in the foreground of the *Adoration of the Shepherds* is strikingly similar to that of Saint Mark in the Art Institute montage. A few other comparisons relate our group of miniatures to the Farnese Hours. For example, the scene of the Annunciation in the borders of the Pierpont Morgan montage duplicates two others in the margins of the Farnese Hours.[38] And the *trompe l'oeil* floral ornament in several of the borders of the Farnese Hours is similar to that in borders in our group.[39]

Art historians in modern times have exercised considerable caution in assigning works to Clovio, a practice that has offered a welcome corrective to the ambitious attributions made throughout the nineteenth century. Scholars have often pointed out that the enthusiasm for Clovio in the nineteenth century was unfortunately not accompanied by firsthand study of many of the manuscripts, which were unknown. With regard to our set of miniatures, however, the hesitation to embrace outright an attribution to Clovio appears to stem not from a full-scale investigation of the now well-documented works but from circumstantial evidence concerning Clovio's presumed activity in the 1570s: he is not known to have worked for any pope, he is thought to have lost his sight at the end of his life, and his later work is shrouded in mystery.

The issue of attributing the miniatures in our group appears in a somewhat different light if we recall that modern scholars have had access only to a limited number of these miniatures, which, unfortunately, did not include the Art Institute montage, as well as the Philadelphia and Texas Evangelists. Now, given the close similarities between the *Adoration of the Shepherds* and miniatures in our group, if we go along with those who reject an attribution to Clovio, it is necessary to postulate simultaneously the existence of a close follower whose work is virtually indistinguishable from Clovio's in the Towneley Lectionary but who is otherwise entirely unknown. There remains another possibility, that of just accepting the attribution to Clovio that persisted until about 1937. Although circumspection is still called for, the rediscovery of the Art Institute montage encourages further study of the late work of Clovio in order to settle the question of the identity of the superb artist who painted the Evangelistary for Pope Gregory XIII.

Appendix

Catalogue of Miniatures and Borders from the Evangelistary of Pope Gregory XIII

1. *Montage of the Four Evangelists.* The Art Institute of Chicago, 1982.438.
     a. Miniatures of the Four Evangelists
     b. Border with Medallions of the Four Cardinal and Three Theological Virtues with the Arms of Pope Gregory XIII
     DIMENSIONS: overall, including mount, 36.7 x 25 cm; border, 34.3 x 24.5 cm; evangelists: Matthew, 7.8 x 7.5 cm (with border, 8.3); Mark, 7.7 x 7.5 cm (with border, 8.4); Luke, 7.8 x 7.8 cm (with border, 8.3); John, 7.8 x 7.7 cm (with border, 8.4).
     PROVENANCE: Pope Gregory XIII (reigned 1572–85), Sistine Chapel, Rome, c. 1572, where it remained until 1798; Abate Luigi Celotti (c. 1768–c. 1846), Venice, his sale, London, Christie's, May 26, 1825, lot 86, as Clovio, to Molteno for £16 16s.; William Young Ottley (1771–1836), London, his sale, London, Sotheby's, May 11–12, 1838, lot 242, as Clovio, to Adamson for £16; Charles Rubens (d. 1935), Highland Park, Illinois, by bequest to his daughter; Katherine Loewenthal (d. 1982), Winnetka, Illinois, by bequest to The Art Institute of Chicago in 1982.
     BIBLIOGRAPHY: T. Julian Brown, "Some Manuscript Fragments Illuminated for Pope Gregory XIII," *British Museum Quarterly* 23, 1 (1960), p. 3, as untraced; New York, The Pierpont Morgan Library, *Italian Manuscript Painting 1300–1500*, exh. cat. by William Voelkle and Gregory Clark (New York, 1985), no. 60, as a follower of Clovio; Martha Tedeschi, *Great Drawings from The Art Institute of Chicago: The Harold Joachim Years, 1958–1983*, exh. cat. (Chicago and New York, 1985), p. 26, no. 2, as Clovio.

2. *Montage of the Four Evangelists.* New York, The Pierpont Morgan Library, M.270.
     a. Miniatures of the Four Evangelists
     b. Border with Medallions of the Annunciation to the Virgin and God the Father and with the Arms of Gregory XIII
     DIMENSIONS: overall, including mount, 41.3 x 27.7 cm; border, 39.5 x 26.2 cm; evangelists: each 7.8 x 7.8 cm.
     PROVENANCE: Pope Gregory XIII, Sistine Chapel, Rome, c. 1572, where it remained until 1798; Abate Luigi Celotti, Venice, his sale, London, Christie's, May 26, 1825, lot 87, as Clovio, to Molteno for £19 86s.; William Young Ottley, London, his sale, London, Sotheby's, May 11–12, 1838, lot 243, as

Clovio, to Knowles for £11 15s.; A. Firmin Didot, Paris, at least by 1873 and likely by 1869, when it appears in Racinet, his sale, Paris, June 10–14, 1884, lot 91, as Clovio, to Labitte; J. Pierpont Morgan (1837–1913), acquired by The Pierpont Morgan Library in 1907.

BIBLIOGRAPHY: Auguste Racinet, *L'Ornement polychrome, cent planches en couleurs or et argent...receuil historique et pratique* (Paris, n.d. [1869–73]), as Clovio; Leonardo S. Olschki, "Quelques manuscrits fort precieux," *La Bibliofilia* 10 (1908–1909), p. 80, as Clovio; Seymour De Ricci and W. J. Wilson, *Census of Medieval and Renaissance Manuscripts in the United States and Canada*, 3 vols. (New York, 1935–40), vol. 2, p. 1417, no. 270, as probably Bonfratelli; Meta Harrsen and George K. Boyce, *Italian Manuscripts in the Pierpont Morgan Library* (New York, 1953), p. 58, no. 103, pl. 73, as Bonfratelli; Brown, "Some Manuscript Fragments" (1960), pp. 2–4, as a follower of Clovio; Harry Bober, *The Mortimer Brandt Collection of Medieval Manuscript Illuminations* (n.p., n.d. [1966]), pp. 61–62, as Bonfratelli; New York, The Pierpont Morgan Library, *Italian Manuscript Painting 1300–1500* (1985), no. 60, as a follower of Clovio.

3. *Five Ornamental Border Fragments.* London, British Library, Add. MS 35254.N.

DIMENSIONS: overall, 38.7 x 28.9 cm; individual borders, left to right on mount: 35 x 3.8 cm; 35 x 4 cm; 35.5 x 3 cm; 35.5 x 3.8 cm; 34.8 x 4 cm.

PROVENANCE: Pope Gregory XIII, Sistine Chapel, Rome, c. 1572, where it remained until 1798; Abate Luigi Celotti, Venice, his sale, London, Christie's, May 26, 1825, lot 88, as Clovio, to Samuel Rogers for £9; Samuel Rogers (1763–1855), Westminster, though apparently not in his sale; John Malcolm of Poltalloch (1805–1893), Scotland and London, between 1869 and 1876, when it appears in the Robinson catalogue, displayed in London, British Museum in 1893; purchased in 1895 and transferred from the Department of Prints and Drawings to the Department of Manuscripts in 1899.

BIBLIOGRAPHY: Sir John C. Robinson, *Descriptive Catalogue of Drawings by the Old Masters, forming the Collection of John Malcolm of Poltalloch, Esq.*, 2nd ed. (London, 1876), App. ii.9 (not in the first edition of 1869); *Catalogue of the Additions to the Manuscripts in the British Museum in the years MDCCCXCIV-MDCCCXCIX* (London, 1901), p. 224; Brown, "Some Manuscript Fragments" (1960), pp. 3–4 and n. 4, as a follower of Clovio.

4. *Miniature of the Crucifixion and Border.* a. New York, Brooklyn Museum, 11.499 (miniature); b. London, British Library, Add. MS 35254.P (border).

a. Miniature of the Crucifixion

DIMENSIONS: 23.7 x 14.7 cm.

PROVENANCE: Pope Gregory XIII, Sistine Chapel, Rome, c. 1572, where it remained until 1798; Abate Luigi Celotti, Venice, his sale, London, Christie's, May 26, 1825, lot 89, as Clovio, to Molteno for £38 17s.; J. B. White to Thomas Wilson (died c. 1865); possibly London, Sotheby's, May 15, 1865, lot 1695; William Horatio Crawford of Lakelands, his sale, London, Sotheby's, 1891, lot 777, to Quaritch; Robert Hoe (1839–1909), New York, his sale, New York, American Art Association, February 15, 1911, lot 2447; given by A. Augustus Healy (1850–1921), New York, to the Brooklyn Museum.

BIBLIOGRAPHY: Henry Shaw, *Decorative Arts of the Middle Ages* (London, 1851), pl. 31, as Clovio; New York, The Grolier Club, *Catalogue of an Exhibition of Illuminated and Painted Manuscripts*, exh. cat. (New York, 1892), p. 23, no. 52, as Clovio; C. Shipman, *A Catalogue of Manuscripts Comprising a Portion of the Library of Robert Hoe* (New York, 1909), pp. 14–15, as Clovio; De Ricci and Wilson, *Census* (1935–40), vol. 2, p. 1196, no. 14, as Clovio; B. B. Fredericksen and F. Zeri, *Census of Pre-Nineteenth-Century Italian Paintings in North American Public Collections* (Cambridge, Mass., 1972), p. 54, as a follower of Clovio.

b. Border with Four Female Masks and with Figures of the Four Evangelists

DIMENSIONS: 35.5 x 26.4 cm.

PROVENANCE: Pope Gregory XIII, Sistine Chapel, Rome, c. 1572, where it remained until 1798; Abate Luigi Celotti, Venice, his sale, London, Christie's, May 26, 1825, lot 89, as Clovio, to Molteno for £38 17s.; separated from the miniature of the *Crucifixion* before 1876, when the border appears in the Robinson catalogue; John Malcolm of Poltalloch, Scotland and London, between 1869 and 1876, when it appears in the Robinson catalogue, displayed in London, British Museum in 1893; bought by the British Museum (with no. 3 above) in 1895 and transferred from the Department of Prints and Drawings to the Department of Manuscripts in 1899.

BIBLIOGRAPHY: Robinson, *Descriptive Catalogue* (1876), App. ii.12 (not in the first edition of 1869); *Catalogue of Additions* (1901), p. 224, as Clovio; and Brown, "Some Manuscript Fragments" (1960), pp. 3–4, pl. 1b, as a follower of Clovio.

5. *Montage of the Last Supper and Two Angels Adoring the Host.* London, British Library, Add. MS 35254.K.

a. Miniatures of the Last Supper and Two Angels Adoring the Host

b. Border with Seated Figures of a Pope, a Cardinal, and Two Bishops

DIMENSIONS: border, 34.5 x 26 cm; Last Supper, 8.2 x 7.5 cm; Two Angels Adoring the Host, 8 x 7.8 cm.

PROVENANCE: Pope Gregory XIII, Sistine Chapel, Rome, c. 1572, where it remained until 1798; Abate Luigi Celotti, Venice, though apparently not in his sale; John Malcolm of Poltalloch, Scotland and London, between 1869 and 1876, when it appears in the Robinson catalogue; bought by the British Museum (with nos. 3 and 4 above) in 1895 and transferred from the Department of Prints and Drawings to the Department of Manuscripts in 1899.

BIBLIOGRAPHY: Robinson, *Descriptive Catalogue* (1876), App. ii.11 (not in the first edition of 1869); *Catalogue of Additions* (1901), p. 223, as Clovio; and Brown, "Some Manuscript Fragments" (1960), p. 3, pl. 1c, as a follower of Clovio.

6. *Miniature of Saint Luke.* Philadelphia, Free Library, MS XXVII:7.

DIMENSIONS: 8 x 8 cm.

PROVENANCE: Pope Gregory XIII, Sistine Chapel, Rome, c. 1572, where it remained until 1798; likely John Rushout, Lord Northwick, Northwick Park (1770–1859), his sale, London, Sotheby's, November 16, 1925, part of lot 129; John Frederick Lewis (1860–1932), Philadelphia, given to the Free Library by his wife shortly after his death.

BIBLIOGRAPHY: Brown, "Some Manuscript Fragments" (1960), p. 5 n. 1, as untraced; C. U. Faye and W. H. Bond, *Supplement to the Census of Medieval and Renaissance Manuscripts in the United States and Canada* (New York, 1962), p. 461 (which lists the call number incorrectly as XXVII:1), as Bonfratelli.

7. *Miniature of Saint Matthew.* London, British Library, Add. MS 49520.

DIMENSIONS: 8.5 x 8.5 cm (with border, 10.5 x 10.5 cm).

PROVENANCE: Pope Gregory XIII, Sistine Chapel, Rome, c. 1572, where it remained until 1798; likely John Rushout, Lord Northwick, Northwick Park, his sale, London, Sotheby's, November 16, 1925, part of lot 129; T. S. Blakeney, London, to the British Museum in 1957.

BIBLIOGRAPHY: Brown, "Some Manuscript Fragments" (1960), pp. 2–5, pl. 1a, as a follower of Clovio.

8. *Miniature of Saint John the Evangelist.* Texas, private collection.

DIMENSIONS: 8 x 8.2 cm.

PROVENANCE: Pope Gregory XIII, Sistine Chapel, Rome, c. 1572, where it remained until 1798; likely John Rushout, Lord Northwick, Northwick Park, his sale, London, Sotheby's, November 16, 1925, part of lot 129; Mortimer Brandt (1905–), New York and Baltimore, no. 1297–4; to the present owner.

BIBLIOGRAPHY: Brown, "Some Manuscript Fragments" (1960), p. 5, n. 1, as untraced; Bober, *Mortimer Brandt Collection* (1966), no. 29, pp. 60–63, as Bonfratelli.

9. *Miniature of Saint Matthew.* Location unknown.

DIMENSIONS: c. 8 x 8 cm.

PROVENANCE: Pope Gregory XIII, Sistine Chapel, Rome, c. 1572, where it remained until 1798; John Rushout, Lord Northwick, Northwick Park, his sale, London, Sotheby's, November 16, 1925, part of lot 129.

BIBLIOGRAPHY: Brown, "Some Manuscript Fragments" (1960), p. 5, n. 1, as untraced.

10. *Thirteen Ornamental Border Fragments.* London, British Library, Add. MS 21412.

    a. f. 50 (nos. 109–110)

    b. ff. 46–49 (nos. 98–108)

DIMENSIONS: a: 109, 34 x 4 cm; 110, 35 x 3.8 cm; b: 98, 36 x 4 cm; 99, 32 x 4 cm; 100, 35 x 4 cm; 101, 35 x 3.8 cm; 102, 35 x 3.8 cm; 103, 34.5 x 3.8 cm; 104, 35.3 x 3.8 cm; 105, 36 x 4 cm; 106, 35 x 3.8 cm; 107, 26.5 x 4.5 cm; 108, 26.5 x 3.8 cm.

PROVENANCE: Pope Gregory XIII, Sistine Chapel, Rome, c. 1572, where it remained until 1798; Abate Luigi Celotti, Venice, though apparently not in his sale; William Young Ottley, though not identified in his sale; Samuel Rogers, Westminster, his sale, London, Christie's, April 28, 1856, part of lot 1002, as from the collection of William Young Ottley; acquired by the British Museum in 1856.

BIBLIOGRAPHY: *Catalogue of Additions to the Manuscripts in the British Museum in the Years MDCCCLIV-MDCCCLX* (London, 1875), pp. 377–78; Brown, "Some Manuscript Fragments" (1960), p. 4, borders on f. 50 as by a follower of Clovio, and on ff. 46–49 as by a related but feebler hand.

Notes

WARDROPPER, "A New Attribution to Francesco Mochi," pp. 102–119.

1. The bust measures 40.5 cm high, 33 cm wide, and 29 cm deep; with its socle it is 69 cm high. It is not clear whether the socle is original to the bust. It was not used to display the bust when photographed in 1917 (see note 15), when it appeared on a stand covered with brocaded velvet. The silhouette, however, is compatible with period socles (see fig. 13), and Mochi is known to have used black marble socles (see fig. 11). Anthony Roth first proposed identifying this bust as Mochi's, and he contributed many ideas in support of this attribution. A number of scholars have generously offered observations on the bust, and I would particularly like to thank Jennifer Montagu, Anthony Radcliffe, and Diane David.

2. Rudolf Wittkower, *Art and Architecture in Italy: 1600–1750*, 3rd ed. (Harmondsworth and Baltimore, 1973), p. 85.

3. Howard Hibbard, *Bernini* (Harmondsworth and Baltimore, 1971), p. 84.

4. In response to the fundamental study by Rudolf Wittkower, *Gian Lorenzo Bernini: The Sculptor of the Roman Baroque*, 2nd ed. (London, 1966), Irving Lavin has made revolutionary contributions ranging from the redating of early works in "Five New Youthful Sculptures by Gian Lorenzo Bernini and a Revised Chronology," *Art Bulletin* 50, 3 (1970), pp. 223–48, to a synthetic analysis of the works' meaning in *Bernini and the Unity of the Visual Arts* (New York and London, 1980). Recent studies of Algardi have been crowned by Jennifer Montagu's *Alessandro Algardi* (New Haven, Conn., and London, 1985). While Mochi still lacks a major monograph, the catalogues published around the anniversary of his birth in 1980 advanced knowledge of his career, particularly *Francesco Mochi, 1580–1654*, exh. cat. (Florence, 1981).

5. See Jack Spalding, *Santi di Tito* (New York, 1982). An excellent recent overview is Anthony Radcliffe and Charles Avery, *Giambologna, 1529–1608: Sculptor to the Medici*, exh. cat. (London, 1978).

6. In addition to G. Fiocco's basic study on Mariani in *Le Arti* 3 (1940–41), M. C. Donati examined Mariani, Maderno, and Mochi in "Gli scultori delle Cappella Paolina in S. M. Maggiore," *Commentari* 2–3 (1967), pp. 231–60. See also A. Nava Cellini, "Stefano Maderno, Francesco Vanni e Guido Reni a S. Cecilia in Trastevere," *Paragone* 20 (1969), no. 227, p. 18f; and Roger Craig Burns, "Camillo Mariani: Catalyst of the Sculpture of the Roman Baroque" (Ph.D. diss., Johns Hopkins University, 1980).

7. These observations were made by Maddalena DeLuca Savelli in *Francesco Mochi* (note 4), p. 40, no. 3.

8. For a discussion of the equestrian monuments, particularly with regard to their recent conservation, see Bologna, Museo Civico Archeologico, *I bronzi di Piacenza: Rilievi e figure di Francesco Mochi dai monumenti equestri farnesiani*, exh. cat. (1986). See also Gaetano Pantaleoni, *Il Baroco del Mochi nei Cavalli Farnesiani* (Piacenza, 1975).

9. See Irving Lavin, *Bernini and the Crossing of St. Peter's* (New York, 1968). Together with Bernini's and Mochi's sculptures, Duquesnoy's *Saint Andrew* and Andrea Bolgi's *Saint Helena* completed the plan for four statues. See also Jennifer Montagu, "A Model by Francesco Mochi for the 'Saint Veronica,'" *Burlington Magazine* 124 (July 1982), pp. 432–36.

10. Irving Lavin, "Duquesnoy's 'Nano di Crequi' and Two Busts by Francesco Mochi," *Art Bulletin* 52 (1970), p. 144.

11. See, for example, C. Gnudi and Denis Mahon, *Il Guercino* (Bologna, 1968), p. 163f; Los Angeles County Museum of Art, *Guido Reni, 1575–1642*, exh. cat. (1988).

12. The *Bust of Cardinal Antonio Barberini* was first identified by Lavin (note 10), pp. 138–39.

13. For the bust, which is in the Museo di Roma, see *Francesco Mochi* (note 4), p. 71, no. 18.

14. Lavin (note 10), pp. 137–38. V. Martinelli, "Alcune opere inedite di Francesco Mochi," *Arti Figurativi* 2 (1946), pp. 72–79, proposed a later dating.

15. Charles Oulmont, "Collection M. F. Gentili di Giuseppi," *Les Arts* 162 (1917), p. 18.

16. See Lavin (note 10).

17. See Wittkower (note 4), p. 199, no. 31.

18. See, for example, New York, The Metropolitan Museum of Art, *The Art of Caravaggio*, exh. cat. (1985), no. 66; or Maurizio Fagulo dell'Arco, *Bernini: Una introduzione al gran teatro del baroco* (Rome, 1967), nos. 40, 248.

19. Ulrich Middeldorf, *Sculptures from the Samuel H. Kress Collection: European Schools, Fourteenth to Nineteenth Centuries* (London and New York, 1976), pp. 23–24, figs. 43–44; John Pope-Hennessy, *Catalogue of Italian Sculpture in the Victoria and Albert Museum* (London, 1964), no. 176, fig. 187.

20. See Mariette L. Fransolet, *François Duquesnoy, sculpteur d'Urbain VIII, 1597–1643* (Brussels, 1942).

21. G. Fiori, "Notizie biographiche di Gian Antonio e Eugenio Bianchi, Francesco Mochi e Giulio Mazzoni," *Bolletino Storico Piacentino* (Jan.–June 1980), pp. 63–75.

22. See Lavin (note 10).

23. Giovanni Battista Passeri, *Vite de'pittori, scultori ed architetti che hanno lavorato in Roma. . .* (1772; reprint, Leipzig and Vienna, 1934), p. 133.

24. C. D'Onofrio, *Roma vista da Roma* (Rome, 1967), pp. 150–53, 415–16. This possibility was suggested by Diane David in a letter to the author.

25. Marilyn Aronberg-Lavin, *Barberini Documents and Inventories of Art* (New York, 1975).

26. Italian by birth, Gentile di Giuseppe lived in Paris early in the twentieth century. He wrote occasional articles on art, such as "A proposito della 'Morte della Vergine' attribuita a Giotto," *Rassegna d'arte* 15 (1915), pp. 187–88. His collection was primarily Italian paintings of the Renaissance and Baroque, but also included northern painting (by Peter Paul Rubens and others), as well as some sculpture, such as a terracotta study attributed to Bernini. Some of his works now in important collections include El Greco's *Holy Family* in the Cleveland Museum of Art, Gentile da Fabriano's *Madonna* in the Museum of Fine Arts, Houston, and two Canaletto *vedutas* in The Art Institute of Chicago (which entered the collection much earlier than the *Bust of a Youth*).

RORIMER, "The Date Paintings of On Kawara," pp. 120–137.

This article is based on an earlier essay published in Le Consortium Dijon, *On Kawara*, exh. cat. (1985).

1. This painting was exhibited in the museum's *73rd American Exhibition*, June 9–August 5, 1979, organized by A. James Speyer and Anne Rorimer, along with other works by Kawara. It was installed next to another painting of the same size, *July 16, 1969, Today Series* ("Neil Armstrong, Edwin E. Aldrin, Jr., Michael Collins"), which was painted on the day of the launching of the Apollo 11 to the moon, as its subtitle (which names the astronauts of that voyage) suggests.

2. Quoted in Gregory Battcock, ed., *Minimal Art: A Critical Anthology* (New York, 1968), p. 157.

3. Quoted in Phyllis Tuchman, "An Interview with Robert Ryman," *Artforum* (May 1971), p. 53.

4. Quoted in Christel Sauer, "Robert Ryman: Introduction," in Zurich, InK. Halle für internationale neue Kunst, *Robert Ryman*, exh. cat. (1980), p. 15.

5. Quoted in London, Tate Gallery, *Piero Manzoni: Paintings, Reliefs and Objects*, exh. cat. (1974), p. 47.

6. Ibid.

7. Quoted in Yves Klein, "The Monochrome Adventure," in Houston, Institute for the Arts, Rice University, *Yves Klein, 1928–1962, A Retrospective*, exh. cat. (1982–83), p. 220.

8. Quoted in Margit Rowell, "Ad Reinhardt: Style as Recurrence," in New York, Solomon R. Guggenheim Museum, *Ad Reinhardt and Color*, exh. cat. (1980), p. 23.

9. Yves Klein, "The War: A Little Personal Mythology of the Monochrome," in Houston, Institute for the Arts, Rice University (note 7), p. 218.

10. See New York, Solomon R. Guggenheim Museum (note 8), p. 26.

11. Klein quoted in Houston, Institute for the Arts, Rice University (note 7), p. 221.

12. Ibid., p. 224.

13. Suggested by the artist in conversation with the author, January 1985.

14. The series stopped in 1979, when the rubber stamp Kawara used on the postcards was stolen from his briefcase in Stockholm. This work may be resumed someday. See Stockholm, Moderna Museet, *On Kawara: continuity/discontinuity, 1963–1979*, exh. cat. (1980–81), p. 105.

15. The beginning/concluding dates vary according to the year in which Kawara started the volumes. *One Million Years — Past* exists in twelve editions, while editions of *One Million Years — Future* are still in progress, eight or nine having been completed.

AMISHAI-MAISELS, "Chagall's *White Crucifixion*," pp. 138–153.

1. See, for example, Fr. A.-M., "Tu ne feras pas d'images," *L'Art sacré* (July–Aug. 1961), pp. 7–8; Jean Cassou, *Chagall* (London, 1965), pp. 240–48; Jean-Paul Crespelle, *Chagall* (New York, 1970), p. 214; Walter Erben, *Marc Chagall* (London, 1966), pp. 112–16; Raïssa Maritain, "Chagall," *L'Art sacré* (July–Aug. 1950), pp. 26–30; Cornelia Süssman and Irving Süssman, "Marc Chagall, Painter of the Crucified," *The Bridge* 1 (1955), pp. 96–117; Hans-Martin Rotermund, "Die Gekreuzigte in Werk Chagalls," *Mouseion: Studien aus Kunst und Geschichte für Otto H. Förster* (Cologne, 1960), pp. 265–75; and Allyn Weinstein, "Iconography of Chagall," *Kenyon Review* 16 (1954), pp. 41–45.

2. For comparisons with Russian icons, see Mira Friedman, "Icon Painting and Russian Popular Art as Sources of Some Works by Chagall," *Journal of Jewish Art* 5 (1978), p. 96. For compositions with compartmentalized descriptive scenes around a main image, see Tamara Talbot-Rice, *A Concise History of Russian Art* (London, 1963), p. 73. This tradition would also have been known to Chagall from Byzantine and Western medieval sources: see Kurt Weitzmann, Manolis Chatzidakis, Krsto Miatev, and Svetozar Radojcic, *Icons from South Eastern Europe and Sinai* (London, 1968), pl. 76; and Paolo d'Ancona, *Les Primitifs italiens du XIe au XIIIe siècles* (Paris, 1935), figs. 12, 14, 31, 54.

3. *Cahiers d'art* 14, 5–10 (1939), p. 152; and Paris, Galerie Mai, *Chagall*, exh. cat. (1940), no. 1. On Chagall's system of dating, see Raymond Cogniat, *Chagall* (Paris, 1965), p. 6; and Franz Meyer, *Marc Chagall* (New York, 1963), pp. 10–11, 599 n. 3.

4. *Cahiers d'art* (note 3); and Paris, Centre Georges Pompidou, *Marc Chagall,*

Oeuvres sur papier, exh. cat. (1984), no. 106. The drawing bears a strange inscription on the bottom, "Esquisse 1937," labeling it as a sketch on the drawing itself, a unique occurrence in Chagall's work. Such information is usually written later on the back of a mount (e.g., no. 104), either when a work is catalogued or when it is sent off for exhibition. The drawing also contains all of the details of the original work, in contradistinction to Chagall's usual sketching method (e.g., nos. 12, 30–32, 35, 37, 105, 129), even when the sketch is a blocked-out cartoon for a painting (e.g., nos. 76–77). It thus seems logical to conclude that the sketch was drawn *after* rather than for the painting. Chagall's practice of making sketches *after* his paintings is amply documented, although this is not always acknowledged (e.g., nos. 38, 100). If the sketch was done at the time Chagall changed the painting, it would also explain his mistake in dating, as though he were trying to remember afterward when it had been painted.

5. Meyer (note 3), p. 414, and p. 609 n. 9.

6. *Cahiers d'art* 15, 1–2 (1940), p. 34. There is no photograph of the painting in the catalogue for this show at the Galerie Mai in Paris (Jan. 26–Feb. 26, 1940). However, Alexandre Benois's review, which accompanied the exhibition photographs in *Cahiers d'art*, suggests (but does not state) that the original details were still visible (see quotation on page 143, cited in note 16).

7. This could have been either before Chagall moved to Gordes in Easter 1940 or during the year he remained there, while the Germans occupied France. During this time, the painting was in his hands.

8. Meyer (note 3), pp. 431–32; and Sidney Alexander, *Marc Chagall* (New York, 1978), pp. 327, 332–33.

9. *Liturgical Arts* 12 (May 1944), p. 65. Although the painting seems to have been exhibited in the United States between 1941 and 1946 (Marc Chagall, "Chronology," p. 3, typescript, Museum of Modern Art Library, New York), I have been unable to find a catalogue listing, a description, or photograph of it preceding 1944. However, it seems unlikely that the changes were made at that date or, in fact, in New York. A pre-New York dating is also suggested by the fact that similar "smudged" "Ich bin Jude" signs appear in other works executed in New York—such as *The Yellow Crucifixion* of 1943 (lower right) and *The Crucified* of 1944 (main figure) (see Meyer [note 3], pp. 456–57; and Lionello Venturi, *Chagall* [New York, 1945], pl. 59)—but there are no photographs to indicate that these signs were altered rather than painted that way from the start.

10. Chagall, "Chronology" (note 9), p. 3; and James Johnson Sweeney, *Marc Chagall* (New York, 1946), p. 62.

11. See, for example, Gerhard Schoenberner, *The Yellow Star* (London, 1969), pp. 18–19; and Fr. Reichentàl, "*Arbeit Macht Frei*" (Bratislava, 1946), pl. 1.

12. *Encyclopedia Judaica*, vol. 8 (Jerusalem, 1971), p. 839.

13. Abraham Walt, "Al Tira Avdi Ya'akov" ("Fear not my servant Jacob"), *Lieder un Poemen* (in Yiddish), vol. 2 (New York, 1938), pp. 284–86.

14. Chagall had just finished his major painting, *Revolution* of 1937, celebrating the Russian Revolution and its aftermath, in which he had taken part as Commissar for Art in Vitebsk. See Meyer (note 3), pp. 392, 412–14.

15. David G. Roskies, *Against the Apocalypse* (Cambridge, Mass., 1984), pp. 32–33; and *Midrash Rabbah: Lamentations*, trans. A. Cohen (London, 1939), pp. 42–43.

16. Alexandre Benois, "Les Expositions: Chagall, Oeuvres récentes," *Cahiers d'art* 15, 1–2 (1940), p. 33. All translations in the text are by the author.

17. L. Leneman, "Marc Chagall wegen zeine Christus-figuren als Symbol fun Yidishe Martyrertum," *Unzer Wort* (in Yiddish) (Jan. 22, 1977), p. 4.

18. Hugh Thomas, *Goya: The Third of May 1808* (New York, 1973), pp. 12–14; and George Grosz, *Hintergrund* (Berlin, 1928), pl. 10. See also Boardman Robinson's 1916 cartoon in which Jesus, the man of peace, is shot as a deserter; and Bohdan Nowak's *Unknown Soldier* of 1930 in D. J. R. Bruckner, Seymour Chwast, and Steven Heller, *Art against War* (New York, 1984), pp. 50–51, 76.

19. Otto Pankok, *Die Passion* (Gütersloh, 1970); and Mario De Micheli, *Guttuso* (Milan, 1963), pl. 6. For a full discussion of this type of iconography, see Ziva Amishai-Maisels, "Christological Symbolism of the Holocaust," *Remembering for the Future* (Oxford, 1988), vol. 2, pp. 1657–71; and idem, *Depiction and Interpretation: The Influence of the Holocaust on the Visual Arts* (Oxford, in press), pt. 2, chap. 3.

20. For the theology involved here and the differences in approach between Christians and Jews, see Ziva Amishai-Maisels, "The Jewish Jesus," *Journal of Jewish Art* 9 (1982), pp. 92–93, 95.

21. Ibid., pp. 93–96.

22. Moses Jacob Ezekiel, *Memoirs from the Baths of Diocletian*, ed. Joseph Gutmann (Detroit, 1975), pp. 21–23. For Ezekiel's reasons for making this relief, see Gutmann, "Jewish Themes in the Art of Moses Jacob Ezekiel," in Philadelphia, National Museum of American Jewish History, *Ezekiel's Vision: Moses Jacob Ezekiel and the Classical Tradition*, exh. cat. (1985), pp. 27–34.

23. Amishai-Maisels (note 20), pp. 91, 96–101.

24. Marc Chagall, *My Life* (New York, 1960), pp. 77, 79–80; and Vladimir V. Stasov, ed., *Mark Matveyevitch Antokolsky* (St. Petersburg, 1905).

25. For a discussion of the journal's influence on Chagall, see Amishai-Maisels, "Chagall and the Jewish Revival: Center or Periphery?" in Jerusalem, Israel Museum, *Tradition and Revolution: The Jewish Renaissance in Russian Avant-Garde Art 1912–1928*, exh. cat. (1987), pp. 73, 78, 80–84, 92–96.

26. Meyer (note 3), pp. 172–75. The dating of this sketch is problematic. Chagall told Meyer, probably in the 1950s, that he had done the sketch in Russia, that is before 1910. Meyer, however, was careful not to date the sketch (ibid., p. 740) because there is no date written on it. Chagall, who was notoriously nonchalant about dating, may have assigned it to the Russian period because he remembered that the subject was inspired by pogroms in Russia. Since the style fits both his work in Russia and in Paris between 1908 and 1912, each possibility is taken into account in the essay.

27. *Encyclopedia Judaica* (note 12), vol. 4, pp. 399–400; and Simon Dubnov, *History of the Jews*, rev. ed., vol. 5 (New York, 1973), pp. 716–47, 769.

28. For the types of saints involved, see Talbot-Rice (note 2), p. 142.

29. Paris, Centre Georges Pompidou, *Marc Chagall* (note 4), p. 74.

30. These details are particularly clear in the sketch for these figures (ibid., no. 35), where the slim shawl with fringes appears to develop from the unfringed stole of Russian church vestments often visible in icons. See, for example, Talbot-Rice (note 2), pp. 142, 161.

31. For the context in which this work was done and a more detailed description of its imagery, see Amishai-Maisels (note 20), pp. 100–101. For other examples of Chagall's hidden symbolism in his paintings at this time and the reasons behind it, see Amishai-Maisels, "Chagall's Jewish In-Jokes," *Journal of Jewish Art* 5 (1978), pp. 76–93.

32. For one possible interpretation of the personal meaning involved here, see Abraham Kampf, "Marc Chagall — Jewish Painter," *The Reconstructionist* 16 (Jan. 12, 1951), pp. 10–13.

33. Zurich, Kunsthaus, *James Ensor*, exh. cat. (1983), pp. 145–47.

34. For the pogrom in Vitebsk in October 1904 and the deportations, see Dubnov (note 27), vol. 5, pp. 728, 768. For Chagall's sufferings as a boy from anti-Semitism, see Roy McMullen, *The World of Marc Chagall* (London, 1968), pp. 77, 142. For his imprisonment, see Chagall (note 24), p. 83.

35. Georges Charbonnier, *Le Monologue du peintre*, vol. 2 (Paris, 1960), p. 45.

36. Bern, Klipstein and Kornfeld, *Marc Chagall*, exh. cat. (1960), no. 14. To compare this landscape with those he did in Peyra-Cava, see Meyer (note 3), no. 577.

37. Dubnov (note 27), vol. 5, p. 868; and Meyer (note 3), p. 381 and nos. 575–78. The context of this drawing is clarified somewhat in an undated sketch in which the Crucifixion appears through the door or window of a room where people are fighting, while the Four Riders of the Apocalypse hover ominously overhead (Meyer [note 3], p. 432).

38. Crespelle (note 1), pp. 207–08; and Simon Schwartz, *La Réhabilitation juive de Jésus* (Limoges, n.d.), p. 181.

39. Edmund Fleg, *Jésus raconté par le Juif errant* (Paris, 1933), p. 299.

40. *The Falling Angel* was first sketched in 1923/24 and painted in 1933, at which time it was exhibited and photographed. The current state dates to 1947, and in it Chagall added several figures (Franz Meyer, *Marc Chagall, Der Engelssturz* [Stuttgart, 1964]).

41. Meyer (note 3), no. 613; Hans-Martin Rotermund, *Marc Chagall und die Bibel* (Lahr, 1970), p. 24.

42. Rainer Zimmermann, *Otto Pankok* (Berlin, 1972), pp. 47–51; and Karl Ludwig Hofmann, "Antifaschistische Kunst in Deutschland," in Karlsruhe, Badischer Kunstverein, *Widerstand Statt Anpassung* (Berlin, 1980), p. 67.

43. Joseph Bonsirven, S. J., *Les Juifs et Jésus — Attitudes nouvelles* (Paris, 1937), pp. 170–72, 199, 203–04.

44. Tokyo, Seibu Museum of Art, *Marc Chagall*, exh. cat. (1981), no. 7.

45. For a discussion of these and related works, see Amishai-Maisels (note 20), pp. 85–86, 90–91, 101–02.

46. Marc Chagall, *Poèmes* (Geneva, 1975), p. 81.

47. James Johnson Sweeney, "Art Chronicle — I — An Interview with Marc Chagall," *Partisan Review* 11 (Winter 1944), p. 91, emphasis mine.

48. Yvan Christ, *Chagall dessins* (Paris, 1953), no. 56; and Rotermund (note 41), p. 133. Rotermund called the sketch *Inferno* and dated it to about 1943 for no clear reason, whereas the very similar sketch in Christ's book is clearly dated 1941 beside Chagall's signature. For depictions of deportations, see Janet Blatter and Sybil Milton, *Art of the Holocaust* (New York, 1981), no. 40; and Amishai-Maisels, *Depiction and Interpretation* (note 19), pt. 1, chap. 3.

49. Venturi (note 9), no. 45.

50. Meyer (note 3), no. 696.

51. Cassou (note 1), p. 249. The INRI had originally been painted under his name.

52. Meyer (note 3), no. 689; and Chagall (note 46), pp. 66, 17, corrected after the Yiddish original in *Die Goldene Keit* 60 (1967), pp. 95, 102. The imagery Chagall used in his second poem is based on Uri Zvi Greenberg's Yiddish poem "Golgotha," written around 1920: "Every morning I am nailed up anew on the burning red cross" (Uri Zvi Greenberg, *Gezamelte Werk*, vol. 1 [Jerusalem, 1979], p. 305).

53. See, for example, Paris, Musée du Louvre, *Le Message biblique de Marc Chagall*, exh. cat. (1967); and Ziva Amishai-Maisels, *Marc Chagall at the Knesset* (New York, 1973).

HINDMAN and HEINLEN, "A Connoisseur's Montage: The *Four Evangelists* Attributed to Giulio Clovio," pp. 154–174.

1. For Vasari on Clovio, see Giorgio Vasari, *Lives of the Most Eminent Painters, Sculptors, and Architects*, trans. A. B. Hinds, vol. 4 (London, 1927), pp. 244–49.

2. London, Christie's, *A Catalogue of a...Collection of Illumined Miniature Paintings Taken from the Choral Books of the Papal Chapel in the Vatican During the French Revolution; and Subsequently Collected and Brought to This Country by the Abate Celotti* (May 26, 1825).

3. A. N. L. Munby, *Phillipps Studies No. 3: The Formation of the Phillipps Library up to the Year 1840* (Cambridge, 1954), pp. 50–51; and idem, *Connoisseurs and Miniature Painting 1750–1850* (Oxford, 1972), pp. 65–67.

4. T. Julian Brown, "Some Manuscript Fragments Illuminated for Pope Gregory XIII," *British Museum Quarterly* 23, 1 (1960), pp. 2–5.

5. On the history of attributions, see later discussion in this essay and the accompanying Appendix.

6. Brown (note 4), p. 5 n. 5, noted that lot 88, which was bought by Samuel Rogers, has possibly, but not likely, been remounted in British Library Add. MS 21412 (see Appendix, no. 10), a collection of leaves and cuttings made up of lots 1002, 1005, 1006, 1008, and 1009 from Rogers's sale at Christie's, London (April 28, 1856). In fact, however, the only borders in Add. MS 21412 that might be identified as lot 88 of the Celotti sale were part of lot 1002 of Rogers's sale, which were said to be from the collection of William Young Ottley, not from Celotti.

7. Harry Bober, *The Mortimer Brandt Collection of Medieval Manuscript Illuminations* (n.p., 1966), p. 62.

8. *A Catalogue of...Illumined Miniature Paintings* (note 2) asserts that these four lots were from a volume "in the Sacristy of the Papal Chapel" mentioned by Baglione in his 1642 life of Clovio (p. 27), but there appears to be no basis for this statement; see G. Baglione, *Le Vite de' Pittori, Scultori, Architetti, ed Intagliatori, dal Pontificato di Gregorio XIII. del 1572. fino a' tempi di Papa Urbano VIII. nel 1642*, new ed. (Naples, 1733), pp. 14–15, which provides insufficient information to identify the manuscript.

9. On the Towneley Lectionary, see Maria Cionini-Visani and Grgo Gamulin, *Giorgio Clovio: Miniaturist of the Renaissance* (New York, 1980), p. 92, with bibliography.

10. As quoted by Brown (note 4), p. 5 n. 6. For further discussion of the content of the inventories, see also Mirella Levi d'Ancona, "Illuminations by Clovio Lost and Found," *Gazette des Beaux-Arts*, ser. 6, 37a (1950), pp. 55–76, esp. pp. 67–68 and p. 76 n. 19. The inventories, dated 1714 and 1728, are now in the State Archives in Rome, Camerale I, Inventari vol. 1560.

11. On the Grimani Evangelistary, see Cionini-Visani and Gamulin (note 9), pp. 99–101, with a complete list of miniatures and further bibliography.

12. See, in our group, for Maundy Thursday, the British Library *Last Supper* (Appendix, no. 5); for Good Friday, the Brooklyn Museum *Crucifixion* (Appendix, no. 4); and for Corpus Christi, the British Library *Angels Adoring the Host* (Appendix, no. 5).

13. The text is from Matthew 5:6–7, "Bea[ti qui esuriunt et sit]iunt iusti[tiam ipsi s]aturabuntur Be[ati misericor]des quonian ipsi misericordiam consequentur." ("Blessed are they that hunger and thirst after justice, for they shall have their fill. Blessed are the merciful, for they shall obtain mercy.") All of the other miniatures from this group have been glued down, so it is impossible to examine their versos for texts.

14. Munby, *Phillipps Studies No. 3* (note 3), pp. 50–51; and idem, *Connoisseurs* (note 3), pp. 65 and 109.

15. Munby, *Connoisseurs* (note 3), p. 65.

16. Suggested in *Hidden Friends: A Loan Exhibition of the Comites Latentes Collection of Illuminated Manuscripts from the Bibliothèque Publique et Universitaire, Geneva*, exh. cat. by Christopher De Hamel (London, 1985), [p. 7].

17. On Ottley, see Munby, *Connoisseurs* (note 3), esp. pp. 62–70. Ottley's publications include *The Italian School of Design* (London, 1823) and *An Inquiry into the Origin and Early History of Engraving upon Copper and in Wood, with an Account of Engravers and Their Works from the Invention of Chalcography by Maso Finiquerra, to the Time of Marc Antonio Raimondi* (London, 1816).

18. We have used the personal copy of the catalogue of one of the purchasers at the sale, William Manson, later of Christie, Manson and Wood. Manson's copy is annotated with prices and the names of buyers and is now in the library at Christie's, London.

19. On Molteno, see E. Manning, *Colnaghi's 1760–1960* (London and Bradford, 1960), n. pag. Molteno's estate sale, which included four miniatures, was held by Christie's, London (March 16–20, 1846).

20. On his sale of paintings, see Munby, *Connoisseurs* (note 3), p. 63. Ottley amassed a collection of more than one thousand miniatures, which were sold at Sotheby's, London (May 11–12, 1838).

21. For an analysis of Madden's views, see Alice H. R. Hauck, "John Ruskin's Uses of Illuminated Manuscripts and Their Impact on His Theories of Art and Society" (Ph.D. diss., Johns Hopkins University, 1983), pp. 104–06.

22. London, Christie and Manson, *Catalogue of the Very Celebrated Collection of Works of Art, the Property of Samuel Rogers, Esq....* (April 28, 1856, lot 1002).

23. On Ruskin's attitudes and collecting, see Hauck (note 21), and James S. Dearden, "John Ruskin, the Collector," *The Library* 21 (June 1966), pp. 124–54.

24. On changes in the appreciation of Clovio, see Munby, *Connoisseurs* (note 3), pp. 25–26; Cionini-Visani and Gamulin (note 9), pp. 25–26; and Webster Smith, *The Farnese Hours* (New York, n.d.), pp. 9–11.

25. On Americans who traveled to the continent to buy books and manuscripts, see Seymour De Ricci, "Les Amateurs des livres anciens en France de 1900 à 1925," *Bulletin du bibliophile* 3 (1926), pp. 2–12.

26. On American collections, including those of Morgan, Lewis, and Ricketts, see Seymour De Ricci and W. J. Wilson, *Census of Medieval and Renaissance Manuscripts in the United States and Canada*, 3 vols. (New York, 1935–40); and C. U. Faye and W. H. Bond, *Supplement to the Census of Medieval and Renaissance Manuscripts in the United States and Canada* (New York, 1962).

27. Martha Tedeschi, *Great Drawings from The Art Institute of Chicago: The Harold Joachim Years, 1958–1983*, exh. cat. (Chicago and New York, 1985), p. 26, no. 2.

28. Brown (note 4), p. 4.

29. Paolo D'Ancona and E. Aeschilmann, *Dictionnaire des miniaturistes du Moyen Age et de la Renaissance*, 2nd. ed. (Milan, 1949), p. 35.

30. *A Catalogue of...Illumined Miniature Paintings* (note 2), p. 23.

31. De Ricci and Wilson (note 26), vol. 2, p. 2077, no. 341, incorrectly cited the miniature of the *Deposition from the Cross* as being in the Free Library, John F. Lewis collection. Lewis had actually given it to Dr. A. S. W. Rosenbach, before bequeathing the majority of his collection to the Free Library.

32. See Cionini-Visani and Gamulin (note 9), p. 92; and Levi d'Ancona (note 10), pp. 66–70.

33. See bibliography in Cionini-Visani and Gamulin (note 9).

34. See Smith (note 24); and for the Uffizi miniature (Inv. no. 812), see Cionini-Vasani and Gamulin (note 9), pp. 67–68, 85, and color plate opposite p. 60.

35. Levi d'Ancona (note 10), esp. pp. 70–71.

36. Ibid., pp. 65–70; the dating is controversial, and opinions are summarized by Cionini-Vasani and Gamulin (note 9), p. 92.

37. For another late work from the "circle" of Clovio after 1556, see the *Triumphs of Charles V* (London, British Library, Add. MS 33733), in Thomas Kren, ed., *Renaissance Painting in Manuscripts: Treasures from the British Library*, exh. cat. by Janet Backhouse, Mark Evans, Thomas Kren, and Myra Orth (New York, 1984), pp. 136–41.

38. Smith (note 24), ff. 54v and 55.

39. Ibid., ff. 36v, 37, 46v, and 47.

MUSEUM STUDIES, *Vol. 16, No. 1*
Aspects of Modern Art at the Art Institute: The Artist, the Patron, the Public

This issue provides an in-depth look at two important works in the museum's collection of modern art: Henri Matisse's magnificent *Bathers by a River* and a moving self-portrait by the German Expressionist painter Lovis Corinth. Other articles examine the remarkable career of Katharine Kuh, the Art Institute's first curator of modern art; the important role of Sergei Ivanovich Shchukin, the Russian collector of French art, in Matisse's career; and Constantin Brancusi's unrealized plans to erect his colossal sculpture *Endless Column* in Chicago.

Spring 1990; 96 pages; 91 illustrations (4 in color); $10.50

MUSEUM STUDIES, *Vol. 16, No. 2*

The essays in this issue examine a diverse group of works from the Art Institute's collection: Edouard Vuillard's monumental painting *Landscape: Window Overlooking the Woods*; a remarkable Chinese jade sheath of the Early Imperial Period; Jean Arp's evocative 1938 sculpture *Growth*; a beautiful German table carpet from the late Renaissance; and the painting *The Vision of Life/The Ghost Dance* by the American artist Ralph Blakelock. The essay on Vuillard is, according to *Chicago Tribune* art critic Alan G. Artner, "required reading for anyone wanting to discover some of the subtlest painting of the turn of the century."

Fall 1990; 88 pages; 85 illustrations (4 in color); $10.50

MUSEUM STUDIES, *Vol. 17, No. 1*
Italian Drawings at the Art Institute: Recent Acquisitions and Discoveries

This issue is devoted to Italian master drawings of the fifteenth to eighteenth centuries: a large sacrificial scene by Gian Francesco de' Maineri; a composition study for Pontormo's *Christ before Pilate*; a pastel-and-chalk drawing by Federico Barocci; Giovanni Benedetto Castiglione's early monotype *God Creating Adam*; and Rosalba Carriera's pastel *Young Lady with a Parrot*. A color-plate section features the Art Institute's drawings.

Spring 1991; 96 pages; 95 illustrations (8 in color); $10.50

MUSEUM STUDIES, *Vol. 18, No. 1*
Kimonos and Ceremonial Robes: Japanese Costumes and Prints at the Art Institute

This issue will mark the Spring 1992 opening of a special exhibition of the Art Institute's kimonos, in anticipation of the reinstallation of the museum's East Asian galleries. The essays in this issue delve into the cultural and art-historical background of these lavish costumes, most of which were intended for use in the Noh theater. This issue also includes an introductory discussion of Noh theater, an essay on the Ryerson Library's collection of books on kimonos, and a survey of a beautiful series of Utamaro prints on the subject of silkmaking. Also featured is a full-color portfolio of all the costumes that will be displayed in the Art Institute's exhibition.

Spring 1992; 96 pages; 95 illustrations (37 in color); $14.95

MUSEUM STUDIES, *Vol. 18, No. 2*
British Art: Recently Acquired Paintings, Drawings, Silver, and Textiles at the Art Institute

This issue focuses on the Art Institute's ongoing effort to enhance its collection of British art. The essays range across a diverse group of recent acquisitions: a self-portrait by Joseph Wright of Derby; a remarkable sketchbook by Edward Burne-Jones; a masterpiece of silver by Omar Ramsden; a dramatic painting by Philippe Jacques de Loutherbourg entitled *The Destruction of Pharoah's Army*; a self-portrait drawing by Simeon Solomon; a group of textiles by William Morris; and a previously unknown drawing by James McNeill Whistler. Also featured is a series of color plates reproducing the principal works covered in the essays.

Fall 1992; 96 pages; 95 illustrations (8 in color); $10.50

All issues of Museum Studies *are available from the The Art Institute of Chicago Museum Shop, as well as from two new Museum Shop locations: 900 North Michigan Avenue, fifth floor, and Oakbrook Center, main level. Art Institute members receive a 10% discount on all purchases at each location. For more information concerning the Museum Shop, call (312) 443-5207.* Museum Studies *is also available by mail from the Publications Department, The Art Institute of Chicago, Michigan Avenue at Adams Street, Chicago, Illinois 60603 (please make checks payable to* Museum Studies*).*